homework

A NEW DIRECTION

NEILA A. CONNORS

NATIONAL MIDDLE SCHOOL ASSOCIATION

nmsa®

National Middle School Association

Neila A. Connors teaches in the Department of Middle Grades Education at Valdosta State College, Valdosta, Georgia. Dr. Connors, a former middle school teacher, is nationally recognized for her dynamic presentations and effective leadership. She is a member of NMSA's Board of Trustees and the Executive Council.

The Publications Committee appreciates her willingness to develop this monograph on an important but largely overlooked topic. Thanks are also extended to the organizations which granted permission for reprinting cartoons.

Cover photography by Todd Yarrington
Cover design by Terry Kammer

Copyright © 1992 by National Middle School Association
4807 Evanswood Dr., Columbus, Ohio 43229-6292
Second printing, April 1993

All rights reserved. No part of this publication may be reproduced or transmitted in any form or by any means without permission in writing from the publisher except in the case of brief quotations embodied in reviews or articles.

The materials presented herein are the expressions of the author and do not necessarily represent the policies of NMSA.

NMSA is a registered trademark of National Middle School Association.

Printed in the United States of America

ISBN: 1-56090-065-2

Contents

Foreword

As middle level schools across America move to implement the "middle school concept," major changes in educational practices are occurring. Faculties and students are being organized into teams. Cooperative learning strategies are finding their way into classrooms. The exploratory nature of young adolescents is being recognized in content and practices.

However, one of the most venerable aspects of American education — homework — has received little attention in this movement to make programs for young adolescents developmentally appropriate and academically effective. Routine assignments continue to be made, usually just before the bell. Students, with a sense of resignation, gather up their several textbooks at the close of school, board the buses, and head for home. In a few cases the homework assignments are attacked immediately upon arrival home, along with a snack. More frequently, they wait till after supper at which time they compete with family activities, television, the phone, and fatigue for its place on the agenda. Some parental prodding is often needed to insure that homework gets moved to the top of the list.

Such a view of homework may be a bit overdrawn and rather negative, but it is not without considerable validity. At any rate, it is clear that homework, its effectiveness, its influence on student attitudes, and its relationship to the middle school concept has not received the attention its place in the educational enterprise warrants.

Homework: A New Direction, provides the information needed by middle school faculties to review, reconsider, and reconstruct the out-of-school assignments that seek to extend meaningful educational activities beyond the school day. Included are materials giving the historical backgrounds of homework, the essence of the literature dealing with it, the perceptions and opinions of those currently involved in it, a summary of the arguments for and against, specific guidelines for developing the needed policies to more effectively direct its use, and a challenge to examine this traditional practice.

The full implementation of the middle school concept will necessitate dealing directly with homework. We have avoided facing it too long. This publication will give us the tool needed to initiate discussion, serious study, and planned actions to reform homework.

John H. Lounsbury, Editor
NMSA Publications

THE FAR SIDE COPYRIGHT 1991, UNIVERSAL PRESS SYNDICATE.
Reprinted with permission

Preface

The practice of assigning homework is widespread, nearly universal — but it is not as universally supported. Opinions, both pro and con, abound regarding this traditional component of schooling. Generally, the arguments revolve around the issue of whether or not homework leads to academic achievement and good work habits. Does the completion of homework give an accurate estimate of the mastery of worthwhile knowledge? Does homework neglect the kinds of abilities needed in life situations — decision making, thinking, speaking, and problem-solving? Should or should not homework be given? How much? How often? At what grades? New answers based on a new examination of questions such as these need to be developed.

When I think of homework, I recall my own experiences as a student, especially during my middle and high school years. I especially recollect learning the art of procrastination by putting off the completion of assignments until the last minute. I remember setting my alarm for 4:00 a.m. and getting up to complete my assignments hastily. I also recall a group of my friends getting together in the morning to copy J.F.'s assignments — she ALWAYS did her homework and she let us copy it. Even worse, I remember distinctly being dishonest to my mother by saying "I don't have any homework" so I could partake in more exciting peer-related activities. Later, I would sneak around my room during the late evening, trying to determine what I had to do and the easiest method of accomplishing it. And if something assigned on Monday wasn't due until Thursday, I'd never think about it until Wednesday evening. I don't think I was the only student guilty of such doings. Very few students during my school days were filled with enthusiasm when they heard those dreaded words from the teacher, "...and for your homework tonight." The same situation prevails today.

All across the country, teachers assign homework, often because of a school board mandate, with very little research to support the practice. In most cases, homework is required simply because it always has been. Most of what we do in schools today is done primarily because of tradition. Homework is maintained because parents and others take the position that "When I was in school we were expected to do homework every night of the week and even on weekends." Unfortunately, such traditions become so ingrained that they are rarely questioned.

Another commonly voiced statement is "If we are to prepare students for the 9th grade and the REAL WORLD, we must give homework in the middle grades." I have problems with that statement for two reasons. First, I become weary of justifying middle level practices on the expectations and requirements of high schools (which are in even more need of restructuring). Second, during early adolescence, each student's day is as REAL to them as it gets. The so-called "real world" that lies beyond the present is too abstract to serve as a motivator. Consequently, the experiences they have in school day-by-day must be relevant and sequential. It is not enough to assign homework just because it always has been, or because the high school teachers give it, or because parents expect it. The issue is much more involved and needs to be explored seriously.

The guidelines set forth in this monograph call for some fundamental changes in this traditional component of schooling. This publication offers a framework for thinking through the issues surrounding homework. It includes research findings, a sampling of professional opinion, and the results of a national survey. Scattered throughout are a few relevant cartoons and a number of student comments on homework — just as they wrote them. The monograph does not offer a single or simple "right way." It is the responsibility of readers to evaluate the contents openly and arrive at their own personal or school decisions about how and when homework should be used. I hope that this treatise will be of such interest to teachers, administrators, school board members, and concerned parents that it will lead to a serious examination of homework practices at the local level. This should cause interested parties to scrutinize present practices and make needed changes — keeping in mind that change is not fatal and that you "do not have to be sick to get better."

A document such as this depends on the support of a great many people. All merit my appreciation. First, of course, are the 1,079 individuals who responded to the questionnaire. Without their participation this monograph would have lacked much of reality and relevance. Primary, too, is my wonderful husband, George C. Sneller, who carefully reviewed and tabulated all responses on the questionnaire, supported and encouraged me throughout, and contributed to the development of Chapter 4. His love and belief in me is greatly appreciated. Another important source of support came from Dr. F. D. Toth, Dean of the School of Education at Valdosta State College. Without his understanding and approval for released time, I never would have completed this project. I would also like to thank two talented and committed graduate students from Valdosta State College who contributed to this monograph through an independent study project: Laura Robertson and Sharon Whitley.

Several friends and colleagues provided me with valuable information during the preparation of this monograph. The first is unquestionably my mentor, John H. Lounsbury, who is always cheering me on and supporting my efforts as well as performing needed editing and rewriting. Others deserving of appreciation are outstanding principals who represent "state of the art" leadership qualities: Jeanette Phillips of Tenaya Middle School, Fresno, California; Preston Shaw of Shrewsbury Middle School, Shrewsbury, Massachusetts; Nick Pike of Desert View Middle School, El Paso,Texas; Bob Spear of Powder Mill Middle School, Southwick,Massachusetts; and Marion Payne of Owen Brown Middle School, Columbia, Maryland.

Finally, I would like to thank all of the young adolescents in the world. It is because of them that our lives continue to remain exciting, extraordinary, and challenging. My hope is that this monograph will encourage the teachers, parents, and administrators of these young adolescents to strive for a more process-oriented, sequential, and relevant approach to homework. It is an age-old practice, but it is in need of a new direction.

June 1991   N. A. C.

Note: Dr. Connors would like to hear from readers concerning their opinions on homework or innovative ways to make homework more educationally productive. Contact her at 5166 Woodlane Circle, Tallahassee, FL 32303 or (904) 562-1959.

SHOE

SHOE COPYRIGHT 1991, TRIBUNE MEDIA SERVICES. Reprinted with permission.

1. What is homework?

The word *homework* elicits a variety of reactions from teachers, students, parents, and administrators. The topic can quickly cause a heated debate. Is homework valid, effective, important? Young adolescents, of course, voice the most calamitous reaction. They view homework as a bore and a chore that interferes with their active social lives. Students typically describe their assignments as "boring," "dumb," and "a waste of time." One student openly flaunted his aversion to homework by proudly wearing a button with the inscription "Homework Causes Brain Damage." Another creative fifth grade student wrote the following note to her teacher:

> Dear Miss Courson,
>
> Please excuse my forgetting my assignments this month. I have a good reason. I'm allergic to hard work. I haven't been feeling very well lately. I knew I was not well when I asked for seconds of the cafeteria's lima bean-and-liver pie. But I've spoken to my doctor who recommended me to stay in bed, drink fluids, and avoid all stressful activities like homework. I'm expected to make a speedy recovery. I'll be back to normal in time to read about five books tonight.
>
> dying but dedicated,
>
> Candace Marie Hinson
> 5th grader

Why does the topic of homework continue to generate controversy while eliciting negative views from students? The answer is plain — it is not certain what relationship its use has to academic achievement and it has not received imaginative attention. Unfortunately, when test scores drop an increase in the coverage of content and the amount of homework usually follows. Both "solutions" are easy to execute and do not require additional funds. In addition, many educators and parents *believe* that increasing homework assignments increases students' achievement. Research, however, provides little support for such a position. Some studies reveal that homework positively correlates with academic achievement while other studies find no significant relationship. So an educational practice based on tradition although lacking a proven research base continues.

HOMEWORK DEFINED

Webster's dictionary defines homework as "an assignment given to a student to be completed outside the regular class period." Homework as defined by other authors is "an extension of schoolwork;" "work that students do on their time after school hours" (England & Flatly, 1985; Theroux, 1988).

Cooper (1989) defined homework as the responsibilities that students fulfill after school. He also noted that assignments completed during study halls, library time, and even ensuing classes were considered homework. Cooper's definition explicitly excluded activities for in-school guided study, home study courses, and extracurricular clubs. Paschal (1984) agreed and defined homework simply as assignments completed outside of the classroom where they were assigned.

For purposes of this document, homework is: work assigned to students during class and completed outside of the class where it was assigned or during non-school hours.

TYPES OF HOMEWORK ASSIGNMENTS

Assignments should reflect more than just a teacher's impulsive decision. Teachers should be aware of the different types of assignments possible and plan stimulating activities that extend beyond the classroom. A hierarchy developed by Lee and Pruitt (1979) provides an excellent model for *classifying* assignments. They set forth four major categories:

(1) *Practice* — given to help students master specific skills and to reinforce material presented in class.

(2) *Preparation* — given to prepare students for upcoming lessons.

(3) *Extension* — given to decide if students can transfer new skills and ideas to new situations. Extension assignments require abstract thinking skills.

(4) *Creative* — given to help students integrate many skills and ideas while producing a requested response. These assignments usually take more time to complete, several days, even weeks.

In developing their four categories of homework, Lee and Pruitt concluded that *planned* and *relevant* homework can be effective. Their taxonomy provides a framework for teachers, and if used appropriately can help students form more positive opinions about homework assignments. However, as evidenced by the research reported in Chapter 4, the majority of middle level teachers assign only practice and preparation assignments.

Teachers who focus on the idea of homework as *enrichment* help students "turn on" to learning. The following paragraphs clarify each level and provide suggestions for *planning* effective assignments.

Practice homework helps students master skills but it is often boring, dull, repetitive, and unimaginative. Students should have the opportunity to apply their learning in a personal way rather than simply completing a ditto page of problems or memorizing facts. Teachers must remember when assigning work that students cannot apply what they do not understand. Practice homework proves helpful *only* when it is used to practice and reinforce skills already *learned in class*.

Teachers that plan homework assignments wisely do not assign 50 problems to students who can demonstrate their comprehension by completing 15 problems. Also, students who have mastered skills should receive enrichment assignments. Every student DOES NOT have to complete the SAME assignment every night. An imaginative way is to allow students the opportunity to decide individually what practice assignment to complete. This encourages students to become responsible learners.

Preparation homework helps to prepare students for an upcoming lesson or unit. Teachers requiring preparation exercises should present them as a challenge to the students. Merely requiring students to read a chapter in their text and answer the questions at the end is not enticing. We know that students will read the questions first, search for answers, and rarely read the chapter in its entirety for comprehension. Innovative teachers can use preparation assignments to get students excited about upcoming lessons. They also use students' suggestions, provide options, and do not always rely on the textbook.

Extension homework calls for students to go beyond the information obtained in the classroom. Effective extension homework assignments require students to produce self-initiated projects. The purpose is to encourage individualized experiences, emphasizing production rather than reproduction. When students apply and analyze information that has been discussed in class better retention of information results.

Creative homework offers students the opportunity to think critically and engage in problem-solving activities. Creative assignments encourage students to delve further into the information presented in class and construct their personal model of understanding. Creative assignments provide early adolescents with the freedom to show what they have learned through analysis, synthesis, and evaluation exercises.

Again, the best teachers consider the types of assignments given and work with team members in classifying and integrating their assignments (discussed in detail in Chapter 6). Ultimately, homework should engage students in meaningful rather than repetitive experiences.

MISCONCEPTIONS

There are many erroneous beliefs abroad that either perpetuate or worsen educational problems. Often misinformed, we make decisions based on myths or misconceptions. Misconceptions are reality for many people; to suggest that a different reality exists is to disrupt their belief system. The following misconceptions represent responses from surveys and interviews of parents and middle level teachers.

MISCONCEPTION #1 — Students who have difficulty completing homework have nonsupportive parents and poor environments. Incomplete assignments do not *always* correlate with nonsupportive home environments. Students from educationally supportive homes, involved with many outside activities, often do not give homework a priority. These students sometimes arrive in classrooms with notes from their parents excusing their incomplete assignments. These often are the same visible and vocal parents that challenge many school policies or practices.

> *Homework can realy be a kids worst nightmare. During school every day kids hate to hear their teachers say the words, "your homework is." The whole class makes a moaning sound. Homework takes up all your time to do fun things when you get home, such as, talking on the phone, riding your motorcycle, or maybe just watching T.V., we have no time to do anything at home.*
>
> *If you don't do your homework you can get into lots of trouble. Once I had to clean up the house one afternoon and when I got done I did not feel like doing my homework. I figured one zero couldn't hurt me, but it made me get a sixty-three on my report card, what did I know? Why, tell me why do we have homework?*
>
> *Jason*

Capable students who are bored by repetitious and "busy work" assignments often ignore homework, banking on their test scores to obtain an acceptable grade. When interviewed, one highly talented student remarked, "The homework assigned in most of my classes is just to please the parents. It is boring and a waste of time. Plus, if I have to, I usually can get it done in the morning before school with the help of my friends."

It is also true that some failing students do not even attempt to complete assignments. It is less damaging on their self-esteem to stay at the bottom by inaction than to try and in all likelihood still fail.

MISCONCEPTION #2 — Homework teaches students good study skills and self-discipline. Educators have the illusory impression that homework plays a major role in helping students become self-directed learners. Cooper (1989) points out that "the completion of homework assignments involves the complete interaction of more influences than any other part of the schooling process" (p. 3). Many homework advocates fail to recognize all of the variables involved in teaching good study habits, organizational skills, and self-discipline.

Teaching students these attributes requires more than simply assigning homework. Students need specific instruction on how to study and organize their time. When asking middle level teachers if they became self-disciplined and self-directed learners because of the amounts of homework received during their educational program one gets interesting results. A large percentage agree that even today they still lack the study and organizational skills necessary for graduate level programs. Individuals interviewed agreed that to obtain adequate study skills and organizational skills is not an easy process and certainly doesn't result from the "discipline" of homework assignments.

MISCONCEPTION #3 — More homework (quantity) means better grades (quality). The philosophy that more is better is not valid with many if not most early adolescents. A review of the literature reveals that research has not validated increased homework as a means of improving grades and that assigning more homework can produce harmful side effects for some students. They become overwhelmed and simply give up. Grades do not motivate all early adolescents.

MISCONCEPTION #4 — Homework correlates positively with academic achievement and increased learning. As suggested previously, innumerable variables affect academic achievement. At the middle level, we are finding that homework can cause additional stress for many early adolescents and negatively impact learning. We also find that students who are unmotivated in the classroom usually have little intention of completing assignments outside school hours.

MISCONCEPTION #5 — Homework provides a positive link between the school and the home — parents want their students to have homework and are supportive. The only way homework can provide a positive link is for teachers to work closely with parents and involve them from the onset. Many teachers are not accessible during homework hours which bothers parents unable to answer their children's questions. Some parents also feel assignments are too laborious, not relevant, and take away from the limited time they have to spend with their children.

> *I've always hated homework because it takes up to much of my time. When my mother tells me to do something, I will say I have homework, but she will know what I am doing. She knows I am trying to trick her.*
>
> *Amy*

One parent, when interviewed, stated "As a middle level teacher *and* a parent I can see homework from different perspectives. For my ten year old, homework is a daily three-hour ordeal. More than half of this time consists of reading the chapters, looking up the "darkened" words, and answering the questions after the chapter. I often wonder what they do in class each day. Since homework takes so long, my daughter seldom gets to pursue her interests during the school week. I feel that homework that takes a middle school child this long to complete causes the child to have a negative attitude toward school — this is true in my daughter's case." Obviously, a positive link in not being forged in this illustration.

MISCONCEPTION #6 — Effective (good) teachers give homework. A math/social studies teacher of 24 years experience in Pennsylvania concisely responded to this myth by writing, "Too many teachers have been duped into thinking that assigning tons of homework makes them master teachers and develops their excellence in education ...BULL!"

There are many excellent teachers that actively engage students in the classroom and fascinate students through exciting strategies without assigning mountains of homework. Teacher effectiveness simply does not correlate with the amount of homework given.

MISCONCEPTION #7 — Not enough time is available in class to teach everything related to the subject. Teachers aware of early adolescents' attention span, thinking processes, and intellectual development realize that students can process just so much information. Students have a tendency to "turn off" the teacher when the information presented begins to overload their brain. Studies reveal that students are capable of holding 7-9 pieces of information in their short-term memory. Furthermore, if that information is not reinforced, it is soon dumped. An integrated or interdisciplinary approach to learning reinforces skills and ideas from one class to the next. Students begin to see the connections of materials presented. Using the lack of instructional time as an excuse for homework reveals a lack of understanding about the learning process.

> *Everyday I take no less than 2 books. It is a real drag having to carry all them books on the bus home. And the teachers give atleast 20 problems everyday and you want time to go watch TV or go out but you can't because you have to get your homework done. Your friends are worse than the homework when you have more than them. They'll tease you and say ah-ha I don't have as much as you!*
>
> *Jennifer*

MISCONCEPTION #8 — Homework reinforces the content presented in class and offers students the opportunity to review the day's lessons. Homework *can* reinforce information presented in class but proves ineffective if it is busy work and lacks creativity. Effective reinforcement involves the thinking processes and should encourage activities that engage students in actually doing something with the information. Also, early adolescents look forward to social and recreational activities after school rather than to time reviewing their daily school lessons. Realistically, education is not the #1 priority for most early adolescents, certainly not after school.

CONCLUSION

Determining the extent and nature of homework assignments in the middle school involves many decisions, some of them controversial. Assignments that enhance thinking, foster problem-solving skills, involve students, and promote an exchange of ideas are not easily created. They take time to plan. The *art* of teaching early adolescents involves engaging them, planning collaboratively with them, and challenging them. The acts of assigning homework, establishing homework centers, and developing system-wide mandates will not promote academic excellence by themselves. It takes a school-wide commitment based on an understanding of early adolescents to make the difference.

A veteran guidance counselor summarized the issue well in the following comments.

> Homework certainly has meaning when assigned for the purpose of practice, preparation, extension, or creativity. What is important to remember, however, is the purpose behind the assignment — what do we intend to accomplish? We also have to remember that for any goal to be worthy, it must be attainable. When we know many students come from environments that make it next to impossible for them to do homework, is it fair and does it accomplish our purposes to make these assignments? I believe that homework does still have a place in education but there may be circumstances that should prompt us to look at alternative ways to provide for practice, preparation, extension, and creativity.

FOR BETTER OR WORSE

FOR BETTER OR FOR WORSE COPYRIGHT 1991 Lynn Johnson.
Reprinted with permission of Universal Press Syndicate.

2. How did homework evolve?

Homework is back in style it seems, and despite what some school-aged children believe homework is not a new idea. Homework has been around for over two centuries. In the early 17th century, children received most of their education at the knees of the "dame," a local housewife who taught the rudiments of reading, writing, and ciphering to the children who lived within walking distance of her home (Spring, 1986). As the dame completed her daily chores, students recited the alphabet, read the Bible, and calculated sums. Upon completion of their morning lessons, they returned home. Students recited to their parents what they had learned at school that day.

During the 17th century, homework served as a necessary extension for the brief lessons taught during the day. Education grew sporadically throughout the 17th century. As school systems were formed in the early 18th century homework assignments became more common. At home, students would memorize catechisms and Bible passages. They also read the journals of their forefathers, writings of political leaders, and teachings of religious leaders where available. It was not until the late 18th century, however, that educators came to view homework as a vital and effective part of the students' education (Langdon & Stout, 1969).

In the early 19th century, instructors began requiring supplementary work, identified as homework, for the difficult subjects of Latin, Greek, and classical reading. Teachers, influenced by an increased emphasis on examination scores, gave students longer and longer "supplementary work" assignments thus bringing about an increased pressure to do more school work at home (Strother, 1984). In the 1860s, teachers began working with the students needing extra help with their assignments.

The practice of "holding students in" from recreational activities for additional assistance was a direct result of paying teachers according to the achievement of pupils on examinations. The higher the examination score — the more pay received.

Views on homework in the late 19th century were related to the predominant learning theories of the time. These theories supported memorization and completion of particularly difficult homework assignments "to strengthen the mind." The mind, theorists stated, was a muscle needing exercise to develop it. Homework *drills* for disciplining the mind were, therefore, enthusiastically supported by teachers and parents (Strother, 1984; Spring, 1986).

Around 1910, articles printed in the *Ladies' Home Journal* and *School Review* openly opposed homework. Critics contended that homework was not supervised properly at home and students often practiced mistakes at home. Furthermore, opponents believed that students were required to carry too many school books home.

The debate shifted, and from 1913 to 1937 it centered more on the effects of homework on students' mental and physical health (Foyle & Bailey, 1988). Something of a culmination of the controversy occurred when the British Board of Education issued a government pamphlet that set forth basic guidelines. The report recommended that students under the age of 12 should not receive homework, while students between the ages of 12 and 14 should receive one hour of homework each day, and students between the ages of 14 and 16 should receive homework for 1 and 1/2 hours each day. In the United States, similar views followed (Strother, 1984).

During the mid-1940s educators seemed less concerned with homework and emphasized the need for more extracurricular activities (England & Flatley, 1985). But when the Russians launched Sputnik in 1957 educators quickly moved to advocate more homework as a means of catching up with the Russians. The term *academic excellence* evolved (sound familiar?) and educators along with parents placed pressure on schools to assign more homework.

By the late 1960s, homework issues took another direction. Some educators were again expressing the view that schools placed too much emphasis on homework to the detriment of social and emotional development. But by 1974 we were in the "back-to-basics" movement and the 1978 Gallup Poll found five out of seven people suggesting that schools could improve by assigning more homework (England & Flatley, 1985).

Lee and Pruitt (1979) became known for their homework-related research during the late '70s. Their taxonomy of homework gained wide acceptance. Their philosophy stressed a planned policy emphasizing the hierarchy of assignments and schoolwide consistency.

In 1983 the infamous *Nation At Risk* report severely criticized high schools for low standards and low levels of student achievement. Homework was included in the attack. The report indicated that time in the classroom was ineffectively used and that two-thirds of the high school seniors surveyed reported completing less than one hour of homework each night. The report expressly recommended that high school students receive far more homework. As a result, many states mandated changes that had dramatic effects on middle level programs.

For some reason, it was *assumed* that if more homework was needed in the high school, more homework *must* be needed in the middle school which prepares students for high school. Many systems quickly put into place homework policies demanding a specific time allotment and number of days per week dependent upon the grade of the student. As quickly as homework resurfaced as an issue, articles began to appear — both for and against — dealing with the question, "Does homework truly affect academic achievement?"

Friesen (1979) reviewed 24 research studies conducted between 1923 and 1979 that dealt with the correlation between homework and achievement. Based on the review, he reported that data neither supported nor refuted the effectiveness of homework. Turvey (1986), on the other hand, reported that studies, overall, revealed that time on homework *did* make a difference in achievement, yet agreed that the literature was inconclusive. Still another review of the literature stated that though the number of valid research studies was limited, their "quantitative synthesis of research studies shows that homework benefits achievement and attitudes, especially if it is commented upon or graded" (Walberg, Paschal, & Weinstein, 1985, p. 79).

Although many people believe that homework increases student achievement, research studies on the effect of homework are still far from conclusive. Epstein (1988) of The John Hopkins University stated that the findings of empirical studies provide contradictory results with most studies revealing inadequate research designs. Epstein further emphasized the need to consider many variables if one is to obtain an adequate understanding of the design and execution of homework assignments. Variables include family background, school organization and policy, classroom organization, homework completion by students, homework return and follow-up, and actual effects on student learning. Unfortunately, most studies are incomplete.

Cooper (1989), in a comprehensive and valuable review of the research available on homework, reported that the role of homework has been minimal in informing parents, teachers, and policy makers. Cooper established that the lack of effect is due to (1) the number and complexity of influences and variables on the effectiveness of homework and (2) valid research on homework would be difficult and costly causing the number of high quality studies to be few. He added that good research would involve the "random assignment of homework and non-homework manipulations to ongoing classrooms for extended periods of time with appropriate follow-up assessments of effectiveness" (p. 5).

SUMMARY

Simply stated, while schools have historically sanctioned and used homework assignments, there has been little data to either support or refute its merit for improving students' achievement. Strother (1984) summarized the controversy over homework as follows:

> Whenever reformers attempt to improve the academic outcomes of American schooling, more homework seems a first step. The justification for this probably has more to do with philosophy (students should work harder) and with ease of implementation (increased homework costs no extra money and requires no major program modifications) than with new research findings (p. 424).

If we indeed want to prepare our early adolescents for the future as self-directed, self-disciplined learners, we must put the past behind us and begin to look at a new direction for educating our youth. The whole concept of homework is a major component of the new direction.

3. The pros and cons

The only commonality that exists when discussing the topic of homework is that EVERYONE has an opinion concerning its worth and purpose. Interestingly enough, in discussions, one quickly learns that people either adamantly favor or strongly oppose the practice as it is usually operated. Seldom does a person remain neutral.

Ideally, teachers and parents would like homework to assist in students' individual growth toward positive self-worth. The main *intent* is to help early adolescents learn to manage their time, to study, and to become self-disciplined, self-directed, independent learners. In addition, *relevant* homework assignments help students with problem-solving, thinking, and organizing skills. Homework, however, becomes *ineffectual* when turned into "busy work"with students going through the motions but internalizing very little.

The authors of NASSP's *Agenda for Excellence at the Middle Level* (1985) agreed that the middle level curriculum should supply students with the skills for continued learning, teach students self-discipline, engage students in productive thinking, and provide challenges. In addition, homework as a component of most middle level curriculums, should attempt to accomplish these same objectives. The report further states:

> To be effective, homework should be coordinated among teachers, related to the goals of the class and the specific topic under study, and should not be given simply to provide additional drill time. Instead, it should require thought, reasonable intellectual effort, the competent demonstration of learned skills, and the acquisition of new knowledge. It should be appropriate in terms of both quantity and quality. The student

should receive specific and regular feedback on homework assignments (p. 7).

The recommendations further emphasized the need for the thinking curriculum to provide students with problem-solving and decision-making situations. Similarly, a need exists for teachers, administrators, and school board members to evaluate present practices concerning the role of thinking in relation to homework assignments.

The pros and cons of homework are almost equal in number. The following section presents both sides of the debate. Citations indicate a research study in support of the statement.

ADVANTAGES OF HOMEWORK

Parents, teachers, and others who favor homework believe firmly that the practice does make a difference. They are convinced the immediate and long term effects make homework worth the effort, even the hassle. In reviewing the literature and the survey detailed in the next chapter, the following purported advantages continually emerge.

1. **Homework teaches students how to organize their time.** Cooper (1989) found that some studies supported this statement and indicated that a long-term effect of homework can be the improvement of students' attitudes toward school with the improvement of study habits and skills. England & Flatley (1985) further stated that students learn how to become self-disciplined and self-motivated as they complete homework.

2. **Homework allows teachers to cover more material during the year.** Turvey (1986) found that homework eased time constraints on the curriculum by extending time available for learning into the out-of-school time. Teachers unable to cover all the material adequately during the class period could have students continue through self-directed learning after school hours. A teacher of 10 years experience wrote, "Homework is essential to develop skills. The curriculum does not allow time to do all the necessary work in class. Discipline and responsibility are also developed during homework."

3. **Homework prepares students for rigorous high school and college requirements.** Teachers continuously stated that students MUST be

given rigorous homework assignments in middle and junior high schools to prepare them for high school requirements. Parents too, suggested that students must be given homework regularly in order to achieve in high school and college.

> *There are two views on homework: Kid's view and teacher's view. From a kid's view, we hate it!!! We do work all day, and then have to go home in our spare time and do more work. For someone with a busy schedule, homework is a MAJOR nuisance.*
>
> *I guess the teachers have a reason to give out homework (besides to irritate kids!) The parents need to know what kind of work you're doing. Sometimes, it takes parents back in time, and you realize they never did well in a particular subject — even though they say they did well. All in all, I guess homework is good for everyone.*
>
> *Kelly*

4.   **Homework promotes creativity through extension and creative-oriented assignments.** Homework provides an opportunity for teachers to create unusual assignments that involve students in activities not possible in the classroom. Homework assignments that give students control over their learning can make a difference. Students begin to see connections to the information learned in school and the world around them (Bradshaw, 1985; Bergstrom, 1985; England & Flatley, 1985; Keith, 1986; Oppenheim, 1989).

5.   **Homework teaches students "how to learn."** Bergenski (1988) supported the position that students who complete homework assignments daily gradually discover the ability to learn material individually and thus learn how to learn. Many teachers responding to the survey indicated that their sole purpose for assigning homework was for the intent of preparing self-directed learners.

6.   **Homework motivates students and thereby promotes learning.** Many educators believe that graded homework is a motivating factor for encouraging students to learn. These same educators see homework

as an activity that students look forward to because it extends learning time into the home (Bradshaw, 1985; Bergstrom, 1985; England & Flately, 1985; Keith, 1986; Oppenheim, 1989).

Homework is a solution to all our problems even though we don't like it, it still helps us a little bit more at home. Understanding homework for some people is kind of a challange. We decide that homework means take the work home and leave it there and then bring it in the next morning, but its not.

Learning to do homework every night is kind of boring because some people like to go out or visit a friend. But teachers and parents say "Homework is more important than getting to go out and play." It took me awhile to understand it but nowI'm on the ball.

Homework is more important than doing anything in your life.

Donna

7.   **Homework satisfies parents who believe homework is an integral component of school.** An experienced teacher said, "One of the biggest benefits of homework is that parents get to see what their child is doing in school. I feel very strongly about the interaction between parent and child at the middle school level and feel that homework needs to be reviewed by parents. Sometimes this is the only link parents have with school at this level." An English teacher wrote, "I feel that homework is *expected* by parents in my district. I would personally like to assign homework less regularly; however, I've found that my turn-in rate decreases dramatically if I don't assign it consistently."

8.   **Homework helps teachers recognize those students who need assistance.** Many comments from the survey supported homework by suggesting that it helps teachers identify students who need remediation. Supporting this position are some studies that see homework as a tool used to ascertain actual understanding of ideas by students once outside the classroom (Bergstrom, 1985; Featherstone, 1985; Salend & Schliff, 1988).

9.   Homework encourages positive school-home communication and involves parents and other family members. A parent from Michigan stated, "Homework can help parents know what students are learning. It provides a good alternative to T.V. and helps develop study skills and responsibility. I am all for it!" Many educators believe that today homework provides the only link between the school and home as there is now so little parental involvement (Bradshaw, 1985; Bergstrom, 1985; England & Flatley, 1988; Salend & Schliff, 1988; Turvey, 1986; Vardell, 1987).   A parent from Florida wrote, "I am a firm believer in homework assignments *every night.* I don't think half of the class time should be given for students to do homework. I think it reinforces what has been taught in class, also gives students a chance to show if they really understand what was taught and could alert the teacher if there are other problems in learning concepts taught."

10.   Homework reinforces and supplements the content presented in class. Homework extends and complements skills, ideas, and material presented during the day's lessons. Homework reinforces and provides practice of basic skills and helps students learn to work independently outside school (Bergstrom, 1985; England & Flatley, 1985; O'Donnell, 1985; Oppenheim, 1989; Salend & Schliff, 1988).   A special education teacher from Wisconsin wrote, "I feel homework, if used properly, can play a real part in the synthesizing and applying of concepts learned in school during the day. At the very least, it gives the student extra practice in a skill and allows parents the chance to review with their child. That is why I believe grading homework is important — if you do work, you want to make sure that someone thought it was important enough to at least discuss or grade." A reading teacher from Pemberville, Ohio further responded, "Homework for homework's sake has little value. Homework for practice or as an extension of a lesson keeps the student thinking and actively involved with the concepts or material being covered."

11.   Homework promotes responsibility, independence, and decision-making skills. Completing homework assignments is important to students' developing a sense of responsibility and decision making skills. The act of completing homework helps achieve goals and foster independence (Bergstrom, 1985; England & Flatley, 1985; Featherstone, 1985; Keith, 1986; Oppenheim, 1989; Turvey, 1986).   An Ohio teacher stated, "I feel that homework is valuable not only as an academic reinforcer but for what it does to teach responsibility.   Being

responsible, setting aside time and effort for independent work is a life skill." A veteran math teacher further stated, "Homework allows a student to think alone in a quiet setting without interruption, hopefully. It presents the student with a learning situation that lets him know if he understands by thinking the problems through. If trouble arises, it at least allows him to know if he doesn't understand."

To me homework is both bad and good.

The reason it is bad is cause the 8th is much harder than any grade I have been in, and the teachers give us to much homework at one time.

The reason it is good, is cause teachers want us to learn and by give us homework, they think it helps our learning ability.

That is what I think of homework.

Rachel

---

12.   **Homework improves grades.** A teacher from a middle school in Florida wrote, "In my 10 years of teaching I have found a direct correlation between doing the homework and scoring higher on exams." Another teacher from Missouri wrote, "Homework increases a student's academic achievement when it is not busy work."

DISADVANTAGES

As with every issue, there are always two sides. Just as the proponents are confident that homework does make a difference, the opponents are just as confident that homework causes more problems than it solves. The following disadvantages are derived from a review of the literature and the survey.

1.   **Homework causes anxiety and frustration in students.** Sometimes students sit down to complete their assignment at home and discover that they do not really understand the assignment or do not understand the concept. If the homework assignments are too difficult for the

student, "learner turnoff syndrome" occurs. Assignments that are too vague or confusing to students are not likely to be completed and tend to create a failure situation (Keith, 1986; Horner, 1987).

How I feel about homework. I think homework is TERRIBLE! Teachers should teach subjects in class, not send assignments home for kids. I can learn more at school than at home. Kids should have a break after school, because they should have their minds on relaxing not work.

Tim

One teacher gave her 139 eighth grade students a questionnaire on homework. When asked, "Has homework caused you any kind of stress this year?" 89% of the students responded "YES". Furthermore, when asked, "Have you ever copied from someone else's homework?" 100% of the students responded "YES". A middle school coordinator stated, "Homework should always be practice of skills previously taught. Students at home should never be at a "frustration level" with an assignment." A parent from Ohio further stated, "I do not feel that homework is essential for a good education. Too much homework creates a negative outlook about school. Children do not have to be frustrated and need time to relax."

2.   **Homework is often unplanned and irrelevant.** Many spontaneous and routine homework assignments are boring for students and do little to promote higher level thinking. When homework assignments are perceived as busy work, students put little or no effort into completing the assigned tasks. Furthermore, such assignments are neglected by teachers. Sometimes students even have to remind teachers that assignments have not been collected or checked.

3.   **Homework assigned over the weekends and holidays takes time away from "growing up."** Everyone needs a break. Homework that is assigned over weekends or holidays interferes inappropriately with students' leisure time. A teacher from Mississippi put it this way. "Homework works great for reinforcement, but when it is given on weekends and holidays it takes away from needed family or together time. Give the children and parents a break on weekends and holidays."

4.   Homework causes students to misrepresent the facts and lie. While we may admire their creative imagination, it ought to be channeled in more appropriate tasks. "The dog ate my homework" is one of the oldest excuses. It is amazing how creative some stories can be. (Some of our readers may even recall the many "funerals" they attended while in college.) Students often prefer lying to admitting that they forgot or just didn't care.

> *I don't care to much for homework because at times it cuts the little day that you have even littler. But it must be very important since parents and teachers pressure you into doing it. I'm going to do all my homework till the day I die, because I want to be a big bisness women. If it takes homework to get me there I will do homework till the cows come home and the fat lady sings. Homework "I THINK I like you."*
>
> *Latassell*

5.   Homework is assigned without adequate collaboration among teachers thereby causing students to have excessive assignments at some times. Overloaded students become frustrated which causes a poor quality of work with little effort given to individual assignments. A parent from Michigan stated, "as a parent of three children, two in middle school, one in junior high, homework is an unending nightmare. Homework is assigned in every subject, every night. It consumes almost every minute of the time from 3:30-11:00 p.m. There is no time for household chores, taking walks, riding bikes, or music practice. This regimen is causing my children to hate school. My husband and I hate weeknights."

A language arts teacher further stated, "Since I am a teacher and a parent, I would like to say that too much homework is a real turn-off! Sometimes the homework load that my children have is more that I could do in one night."

6.   Homework is often not reviewed or commented on by the teacher. Some teachers require homework almost every night for every class yet rarely peruse the papers personally. They seem more concerned with quantity than quality. When teachers do not take the time to review

assignments, students question its relevance. Every assignment does not have to be graded but it should be dealt with in some way (England & Flatley, 1985).

A social studies teacher stated, "If homework is not graded consistently, then the students will not make an effort to complete it and will take it lightly." Another social studies teacher succinctly summarized the situation as follows, "If homework is worth assigning and having students do it, then it should be reviewed and evaluated in some way, but too often it isn't."

7.   An environment conducive for homework is not always available. Unfortunately, but realistically, many homes exist wherein homework is not supported or supervised. Consequently, students do not have the reinforcement of parents to remind them to do their homework. Results from the teacher survey mentioned earlier showed that 54% of eighth graders (n=139) responded "NO" when asked, "Do you have a special place to do your homework?"

A teacher in California expressed these views. "The students that I work with are high-risk. Most have severe dysfunctional families. In these circumstances homework is not a high priority. Survival is — will there be food? will I get beat up? will my parents be drunk? etc. Therefore, I do not add stress to my students by requiring homework. It would not get done in most cases anyway." A guidance counselor from Georgia responded, "I feel strongly that in today's world many students go home to atmospheres where homework is impossible to complete. Homework should never count so much that not doing it would fail a student. Students must be looked at as individuals. If a child is having problems completing homework, a referral to the school counselor or social worker may be needed."

8.   Homework is assigned at the end of class with no time for clarifying purposes or explanation. Early adolescents know when a class period is coming to an end. They begin "packing up" and their thoughts are focused on the upcoming hallway encounters not the final words of the teacher. Assignments given hurriedly during the last few minutes of class are very likely ignored or misunderstood. They result in incomplete, late, and copied assignments (Keith, 1986; Lee & Pruitt, 1979; Turvey, 1986).

9.   Homework results in some students arriving at school without the necessary materials for class. Even students conscientious enough to take textbooks and notebooks home to complete assignments can be forgetful. They and others are likely to arrive at class with the wrong book, no notebook, and no assignment. Teachers then become frustrated and have to find additional materials as well as alter their plans.

10.   Homework is counted as a major part of the grade. Some students are not given a fair chance when a major portion of their grade is dependent upon homework. However, many teachers place that much emphasis on homework. An experienced math teacher in Michigan stated, "Homework is my main criteria for grading. Homework teaches responsibility, organization, and sense of achievement — all parts of the real world."

> *Most of the time, I hate homework. But believe it or not, sometimes I like homework. When I have a low average, I do a lot of homework so it will bring it up. Of course, if I don't do it, it will bring my average down. I have different feelings about different subjects of homework. I like Math and Eniglish homework, but I hate Science and Social Studies homework. Overall, I'd say it really doesn't matter how I feel about homework because I'll have to do it anyway.*
>
> *Josh*

11.   Homework is not a priority with many students and their parents. Students who are actively involved in many school and outside activities are quite likely to put homework near the bottom of the list. And parents who enroll their children in a plethora of activities often do not see the relevance of homework. Unfortunately, when an assignment is not completed, these same parents may write a note to the teacher excusing the child.

Parents, as we all know, occasionally complete larger projects for their children in order to assure a good grade. Science and Social Science Fairs, due to the enormous pressure of competition and status attached, lead many parents to actually complete much of their child's responsibilities. Busy parents may also react negatively to homework.

One such parent stated bluntly, "I think that teachers want too much help from parents. This is a two career world and my career is not teaching. I believe I can decide quality time with my children without the teachers sending home work that should be taught at school."

12.   Homework is used as punishment. Academic activities should not be used for purpose of discipline. Students only learn to be responsible for their own behavior when the disciplinary actions or consequences relate directly to their misbehavior. Using homework as punishment defeats its proper purpose and turns students off — yet it is done. Students, then, begin to associate all homework as punishment. (Partin, 1986; Phi Delta Kappan, 1989).

A language arts teacher agreed by stating, "Homework — especially writing assignments — should not be given as punishment. That teaches children that writing is something to dread. They begin to see writing and homework as punishment." A special education teacher elaborated on this view — "In special education, homework is assigned to complete unfinished daily work, for research purposes, for studying prepared study guides, or for social interaction with peers and parents. Homework should not be busy work or given without a specific purpose in mind. I try to parallel my own work and homework ethics to my students by comparing my job to theirs; and that when I need to complete an unfinished task or do research — I do it and so should they. I would not appreciate homework given to me as punishment or busy work so I try not to punish my students either."

SUMMARY

For every statement in support of homework an opposite one can be found. It is important for educators to realize all of the variables and factors involved. For homework to be successful and correlate positively with achievement, many components must be addressed. Simply completing routine assignments is not enough.

A Georgia middle school teacher summarized the issue when he wrote,

In the 4th, 5th, and 6th grade, students need to develop the "homework habit" — being responsible for completing an assignment for the next day. Developing the trait is more important than the actual content (which should always be review of a skill already learned). Homework shouldn't be so complex as to require assistance but parental review should be encouraged. I have strong feelings about homework. One of the most critical problems we face is that students do not complete homework.

I feel there are three key goals that we need to have well developed by the time students go to high school. One is the homework habit — getting used to having something to complete at home. Second, students should have a place at home where they can be alone to work. The earlier these logistics are worked out, the more painless the process will be. Third, parents need to know what skills are being taught and should reinforce them at home. Homework provides for parent involvement and communication. It's imperative they go over homework — to identify concepts that aren't understood, and for reinforcement of progress. Equally important, the teacher can identify students who aren't doing homework and need some type of help to solve whatever problem is preventing its completion. The primary concern should not be punishing or giving zeros to students who don't get it done, but rather to remediate what is a study skill deficiency.

Homework is simply no open and shut case. School faculties need to review their current practices, reassess the reasons for assigning homework, and determine how current practices effectively fit into the teaching and learning of our middle school students.

4. *And the survey says...*

Since everyone, it seems, has an opinion about the topic of homework and are willing to express it, a survey was conducted to determine the variety of people's perceptions. How divided are they? Do teachers' perceptions differ from those of parents? Does subject taught or years of experience seem to affect views? These are some of the questions the survey sought to answer — and the results proved interesting.

Prior to dissemination, the questionnaire was sent to all members of National Middle School Association's Board of Trustees for refinement. Suggestions were incorporated and the refined instrument was distributed at the 1989 NMSA conference. Copies were also sent to members of the NMSA's Board of Trustees for distribution to their state affiliates. In addition, copies were distributed at approximately 50 workshops nationwide and to the one hundred eighty middle schools in Georgia. (See Appendix A for copy of the survey instrument.)

One thousand seventy-nine (1,079) survey instruments were returned and tabulated. Responses came from individuals in 22 states (Alabama, Arizona, California, Connecticut, Florida, Georgia, Illinois, Indiana, Kansas, Maryland, Massachusetts, Maine, Mississippi, Michigan, Montana, Ohio, Pennsylvania, Texas, Vermont, Virginia, Washington, Wisconsin) and Ontario, Canada. Specific schools represented a diverse population of urban, rural, and suburban school settings.

The survey instrument requested that not all items be completed by all respondents. Questions fourteen through seventeen were to be answered by "persons presently teaching and assigning homework." In entering the data, all responses were recorded exactly as they were reported. Almost three-fourths of the respondents were female.

Positions held by those who returned completed instruments are indicated in Table 1.

The total years of experience teaching early adolescents by the respondents exceeded 12,500 years with an average of thirteen years of experience at the middle level.

Table 1
Percent of Respondents by Position

POSITION	NUMBER	PERCENT
Teacher	823	80.53
Administrator	82	8.02
Parent	50	4.89
Professor	7	.69
Guidance Counselor	17	1.66
Media Specialist	14	1.37
Student	29	2.84

An analysis of the data was performed to determine if the number of years teaching early adolescents had an affect on the perceived daily amount of time students should spend on homework. Teaching experience, however, had no discernable effect on the amount of time. The results of the survey are presented question by question, sometimes supplemented by tables in order to include pertinent details.

QUESTION 1. **Do you feel that students should be given homework? (Next to each grade level please specify the total number of minutes per night the student should be working on all homework assignments.)**

Not surprisingly, the higher the grade the greater the belief that homework should be given and an increasing amount of time expected.

When the responses were tallied by subject-area of teachers no significant differences were noted. Math teachers, however, did have slightly higher expectations.

	Table 2		
	All Respondents		
Grade	No	Yes	Avg Min
4th	10%	90%	32
5th	5%	95%	38
6th	3%	97%	49
7th	2%	98%	61
8th	2%	98%	70

In comparing the opinions of teachers versus non-teachers, very little difference was noted. The overwhelming majority of all respondents (96%) believed homework should be given and recommended roughly comparable amounts.

QUESTION 2. Do you feel that students should have homework on weekends? On holidays? Every night (Monday through Thursday)?

Students, not surprisingly, were strongly against homework on holidays but many saw it as legitimate "sometimes" on weekends and even every night, Monday through Thursday.

Subject area teachers indicated that homework should be assigned over weekends sometimes but very seldom on holidays. A bare majority of teachers thought that homework should be given each night Monday through Thursday. Math teachers supported giving homework on a Monday-Thursday basis at a slightly higher level. Many of them commented that homework should be consistently assigned every day to, as one put it, "mold the students into a pattern or rhythm to get them accustomed to expecting homework on a regular basis."

QUESTION 3. Do you think that parents should help their children with their homework assignments?

"Sometimes" was clearly the favorite response of all groups, especially among parents. The "no"response was infrequently checked.

QUESTION 4. Do you think that all students in a class should do the same assignment?

When all respondents were included, 34% answered in favor of each student having the same assignment, 20% against and 46% felt that all should have the same assignment sometimes.

QUESTION 5. Do you think that students should exchange papers and grade them?

The majority of respondents indicated that papers should be exchanged "sometimes." However, those not selecting "sometimes" more frequently chose "no" than "yes." Parents were the least supportive of the practice.

If students *do* exchange papers, teachers must consider all the variables. Is it being done simply to save the teacher's time? Does the exchange take up too much class time? Does the insecure student feel threatened? Do students pay more attention to the results of their own paper than the paper they are grading?

QUESTION 6. Do you think that every assignment should count as a grade?

The results indicated that, in the opinion of most, every assignment should not be counted as a grade. While the majority commented that homework should be reviewed and discussed, not all thought that every assignment should count on a grade. Some teachers commented that homework should simply be practice the student does to assure mastery of lessons presented in the classroom and is not reflective of achievement. Others indicated that by grading all homework assignments they could assess their effectiveness in presenting and explaining material and also become aware of students' weak points. Students, interestingly, more often than teachers and every other group, thought homework assignments should count as grades.

QUESTION 7. Should teachers personally review, grade, and comment on homework assignments?

Parents gave the highest positive response to this question (45%). Reading teachers were the most adamant against the practice (46%). The range that homework should be reviewed, graded, and commented upon "sometimes" went from a low of 32% (science teachers) to a high of 61% (guidance counselors).

QUESTION 8. Should homework assignments be coordinated with other teachers in the same grade to avoid "homework overload?"

The vast majority of respondents (62%) indicated that homework should definitely be coordinated among teachers so that students are not overloaded on a particular night. Guidance counselors and administrators were the strongest supporters of coordination (91% and 94% respectively) with parents not far behind. Science and social studies teachers were less inclined to feel that coordination was important, although almost half of them did support the practice.

QUESTION 9. How much should homework count toward the final grade in the class?

Overall, 44% of the teachers thought that homework should count from 21% to 30% of the final grade. Table 3 gives percentages of the various groups of respondents indicating their perceptions on how much homework should count toward the final grade.

Table 3 Recommended Percent of Grade Allotted to Homework			
0-20%	21-40%	41-60%	61-100%
Teachers, all 28	51	17	4
Math 29	56	12	3
Reading 43	48	9	0
Science 24	51	21	4
Social Studies 25	53	17	5
LA/English 37	45	15	3
Administrative 45	41	14	0
Parents 11	54	31	4
Professors 84	0	0	8
Counselors 30	50	20	0
Media Specialists 0	75	17	8
Students 7	24	17	52
Overall Avg. 27	49	18	6

QUESTION 10. Should students be punished if they do not complete homework assignments?

After reviewing the responses to this question it was determined that the question did not elicit the type of response intended. Respondents frequently did not answer the question but made a note in the margin asking "What is the meaning of *punish*? " The question should have been worded.... Should students be penalized if they do not complete homework assignments?

QUESTION 11. Should homework be used for punishment? Extra credit? Slow students only?

Eighty-two (82) percent indicated "no" to the question of using homework as punishment, seventy-seven percent (77%) said that homework should be used for extra credit when the "yes" responses were combined with the "sometimes" responses. Reserving homework only for slow students received very little support.

QUESTION 12. Should homework be corrected? Reviewed/graded in class? Planned? Reviewed/explained thoroughly during the class time? Displayed?

The overall response to the question "*Should homework be corrected?*" was 65% "always." Parents and reading teachers felt the strongest while 85% social studies teachers were the least inclined to feel that homework should always be corrected.

The large majority (almost 70%) of math teachers felt that homework should always be reviewed/graded in class as opposed to an overall response of 46% indicating that it should always be done.

"Sometimes" was the preferred response of most groups on the question, *"Should homework be planned?"* Seventy-seven percent (77%) of all responding felt that homework should always be planned. The groups with the strongest opinions for always planning homework were administrators (93%), media specialists (92%), and guidance counselors (90%). The groups placing the least emphasis on planning homework were students (58%) and science teachers (71%).

On the question, *"Should homework be reviewed/explained thoroughly during class time?"* approximately two-thirds felt that this should always be done. Math teachers felt the strongest (77%) and students had mixed feelings with 58% stating "Always" and 42% indicating "Sometimes."

When considering the question, *"Should homework be displayed?"* 87% of all respondents indicated that it should be displayed sometimes. Students responded "never" far more frequently than any other group.

QUESTION 13. Do you think that completing homework increases a student's academic achievement?

The teachers surveyed believe that homework does increase a student's academic achievement;   78% said "yes" and 21% said "sometimes," leaving only 1% responding in the negative. Parents said "yes" to the tune of 81% with the remaining 19% saying "sometimes." Sixty percent (60%) of the students answered affirmatively on this question. The lack of research to support these beliefs on the academic efficacy of homework seem not to have affected opinions.

(Note: Questions 14-17 were answered only by those currently teaching.)

QUESTION 14. Do you coordinate homework with other teachers?

Only thirteen (13) percent of the teachers responded "yes." Forty-three (43) percent checked the "sometimes" category. Reading teachers were the least likely to coordinate assignments with other teachers. It seems clear that coordinating assignments is definitely not a routine practice in today's schools although widely recognized as desirable.

Is it too difficult to coordinate? Does it take up too much time? Are team members not communicating? There are many reasons why the coordination of homework assignments doesn't happen. Some may feel that it is important to coordinate homework assignments but it's just too hard to do with all the other activities and duties required of teachers. Some of the reasons for this condition will be discussed later in this chapter.

QUESTION 15. What type of homework assignment do you assign most often — practice, preparation, extension, or creative?

The responses to this question were predictable; the nature of the subject area determining in large measure the necessary use of *practice* and the potential for use of *extension* and *creative* type assignments. Math teachers by far were the heaviest users of *practice* while social studies teachers were most likely to use *preparation*. ("Read chapter ___ tonight and we'll discuss it tomorrow.")

Table 4 gives the specific breakdown of types of assignments given by major subject areas.

	Table 4 Types of Homework Assignments Given As Percentages			
	Practice	Preparation	Extension	Creative
All teachers	49%	15%	24%	12%
Math teachers	80%	6%	11%	3%
Reading teachers	38%	8%	36%	18%
Social studies teachers	29%	35%	29%	7%
Language Arts teachers	46%	10%	26%	18%
Science teachers	38%	26%	30%	6%

QUESTION 16. Do you assign "group homework assignments?"

Responses to this question seemed to be evenly divided between "no" (42%) and "sometimes" (46%). Only 12% of all respondents checked "yes."

QUESTION 17. Approximate the percentage of students, per class, that complete homework assignments on time.

The overall teacher response to the average percentage of students completing homework on time was 59%. Of the math teachers responding, 76% indicated that their students turned in homework on time more than 75% of the time. Of the more than 1,000 teachers responding, only 42 claimed that their students completed and turned in homework 100% of the time.

SUMMARY

The results of the survey generally support the previously stated generalization: there are many varying thoughts about the place of, the amount of, and the use of homework. The vast majority of respondents agreed that homework should be given; that the amount given each night should progressively increase as the student moved through the grades; that homework should be coordinated between teachers; and, that homework should not be used for punishment, or only for slow students. There was not as much agreement about the type of homework that should be assigned (practice, preparation, extension, and creative), and whether or not homework should be reviewed and graded in class. The belief that homework increases a student's academic achievement is generally held.

While most respondents subscribed to the notion that homework should be coordinated with other teachers, the majority did not do so. Reasons given for the lack of coordination focused on the limited time available to develop a strategy for coordinating assignments.

Throughout the survey whenever the question gave "sometimes" as one of the choices, it was the most likely to be chosen. This could lead one to believe that most of the people responding had no strong feelings about the question one way or the other or saw "sometimes" as an easy and acceptable middle ground position.

When the results were analyzed to see if the years of teaching experience made a significant difference in the perceived amount of time needed to be spent on homework the results indicated that the years of experience teaching made no difference.

In comparing the various subject areas taught, it was clear that math teachers believed in and employed homework more often than any other group. In reviewing the comments, math teachers stressed the importance of getting students in the habit of completing homework. They also stressed the importance of grading, reviewing, and explaining homework more than other subject area teachers.

After analyzing 1,079 responses from professionals whose combined years of experience totaled 12,500 years, it is concluded that little consensus exists as to the role homework should play in the education of young adolescents. While teachers continue to favor homework they rely heavily on the *practice* and *preparation* types of homework. It is also clear from the comments made that few educators have dealt seriously enough with this component of education; the traditional ideas about it, both pro and con, are verbalized with little analysis, citation of research, or probing questions.

SHOE

SHOE COPYRIGHT 1991, TRIBUNE MEDIA SERVICES. Reprinted with permission.

5. Developing guidelines for homework

Research really does not demonstrate that homework makes a difference in achievement. Only when certain conditions are met does homework actually impact positively students' achievement — and those conditions rarely prevail. The advantages and disadvantages of homework in the middle grades seem to cancel one another out. So where do we go from here?

If we really want to make a difference at the middle level, we must stop mandating practices based solely upon tradition and the expectations of others. Second, we must look at K- 12 practices and plan appropriate sequential programs. Too many systems quickly adopt a homework policy as a response to concerns about student achievement. Such policies usually mandate a specific number of days and/or amount of time per week for outside assignments without sufficient study of present practices, beliefs of the teaching staff, or input from parents, not to mention the students themselves.

Homework should be a planned, sequential activity that begins in the elementary grades. During the early years (grades 3-5) students should be taught beginning level skills necessary to accomplish most homework. Students would then be helped to extend those skills so that they could complete more complex assignments throughout their middle years and on into high school. In many cases, students are expected to complete homework although lacking the prerequisite skills. This is like expecting students to speak a foreign language without ever teaching them the language.

An eighteen year veteran teacher stated her firm views thusly:

I strongly believe in homework as a means of developing responsibility. I also believe the student should only have short assignments in elementary school. Equally strongly do I feel that if I assign work, the student deserves my response and immediate feedback. I am very opinionated re: homework! These opinions have evolved through the years and my present stance is strongly influenced by cooperative workshops our fifty teachers attended the last two summers. There we were encouraged to develop the "homework mind-set" before students hit middle school. I've responded to that with homework assignments, short in length, as relevant to academic areas as I can make them, on Monday-Thursday only!

You see, my opinions are colored by my experience as a parent also. I know the parental response to the Sunday night announcement, 'Oh no, I've got _____to do for homework!' I believe one vital part of our American work ethic is work first, play afterward. So a little homework Monday-Thursday, and then different experiences on the weekend."

Educators must continually examine the direction, purpose, and procedures necessary to implement homework effectively in schools. Also, any plan developed must involve the entire system if the ultimate goal is to teach organization, study skills, and self-directed learning. Consequently, this chapter will provide a set of guidelines for developing a homework plan followed by examples of plans presently being implemented. The recommended steps are by no means the only way. In this document, the term **"homework plan"** will be used rather than homework **"policy."** Often, written policies become rigid. The more requirements are put in writing, the more inflexible the policy becomes. Yet, a common key to successful middle schools is *flexibility*.

SYSTEM-WIDE HOMEWORK PLAN

Too frequently we talk about articulation and transition-in/transition-out, but have no organized plan for dealing with these topics. If educators are to provide students with effective practices in the middle school, they must look at the entire system, K-12. Systems that recognize the importance of students are willing to take time to evaluate every practice with the needs of students in mind. A major strand that must be considered when looking at homework is consistency and progressive skill development beginning in the elementary school. As previously pointed out, students cannot apply what they do not understand. A plan that emphasizes *process oriented learning* rather than *product oriented learning* is indeed a plan based on the needs of our students.

The following six steps for developing a system-wide plan are based on a review of the literature, supplemented by recommendations from respondents to the survey:

1. Appoint a system-wide Homework Advisory Team.

2. Collect data regarding the perceptions of teachers, administrators, parents *and* students.

3. Assess conditions that positively or negatively affect homework.

4. Implement a "skills across the curriculum" approach for K-12.

5. Develop a system-wide homework plan focusing on sequential skill development.

6. Evaluate the overall effectiveness of the homework improvement effort and report the results to all affected groups.

These six steps are described in some detail below.

STEP 1. Appoint a system-wide Homework Advisory Team (HAT). The Homework Advisory Team oversees the process, provides support to the schools, and assesses the overall plan. The committee must represent equally elementary, middle, and high school teachers. Interested administrators, parents, school board members, and students should also be included.

STEP 2. Collect data regarding the perceptions of teachers, administrators, parents, and students. The advisory team's first task is to develop questionnaires by which the *perceptions* of these groups can be ascertained. The questionnaire for parents should include requests for information about home support and involvement. The return rate itself from the parents will provide some sense of the home support. The questionnaire for teachers should request information pertaining to: perceptions, amounts of homework given at each grade level, grading policies, review techniques, planning procedures, collaboration, and expectations. (See Appendix A for a sample questionnaire)

The instrument for administrators should request information pertaining to: perceptions, philosophy, expectations, and present requirements. The questionnaire for students should request information about: perceptions, study environment, learning styles, and related attitudes toward studying, time management, self-direction, self-discipline, and organization.

The HAT should be responsible for developing and disseminating the questionnaires and analyzing the results. At the same time, the HAT will be assessing present practices in the system, including an overview of the homework requirements and expectations at different grade levels.

STEP 3. Assess conditions that positively or negatively affect homework. The HAT reviews the demographics of the community, analyzes home environments, bussing routes, drop-out rates, grades, retention rates, and other factors that relate to student achievement. The HAT also should seek to assess school environments and philosophies to determine what opportunities exist for students to become self-directed learners. Successful practices that are ensuring success for all students would be thoroughly reviewed and considered.

STEP 4. Implement a "skills across the curriculum" approach for K-12. The HAT reviews the ways students are taught the skills necessary to complete homework. The team reviews skills introduced and reinforced at each grade level beginning in the elementary school. Skills reviewed may include note-taking, organizing, decision-making, studying, test-taking, problem-solving, researching, thinking, reading, writing, speaking, and listening.

STEP 5. Develop a system-wide homework plan focusing on skill development. The HAT should develop a sequential plan for a "skills across the curriculum" approach to learning. The team must determine what skills are necessary to become a self-directed learner, at what grade level certain skills should be introduced, and how to provide reinforcement from one grade to the next. If a middle school wants to make a difference with students, the help of elementary and high school teachers is imperative. Therefore, a system-wide homework plan must be sequential and planned so that students are prepared for each level of their educational experience. The plan must be *flexible* and *general* enough to allow individual teachers and teams to plan creative homework assignments. The role of the HAT is to provide *guidelines*. Individual schools will and should determine the specifics.

Suggested guidelines for system-wide plan

The guidelines can include a system-wide philosophy concerning homework based on the data collected throughout the process. While reflecting a clear plan and basic consensus, the guidelines must not be too rigid and inflexible lest they be ignored. The main purpose of system-wide guidelines is to provide an overview of the skills to be initiated at each level while leaving the remainder of the decisions up to individual school-wide committees.

The main emphasis for students in grades 3-6 would be an introduction of the skills determined as necessary by the HAT. The guidelines would recommend that assignments in the early grades be short, yield a high success rate, teach students to be responsible, plan their time, and begin to learn how to learn rather than being simply drill exercises. Homework assignments would request the support of adults in the home. A committee within the school would look more closely at students' specific needs and build in other forms of enhancement.

The guidelines would further recommend that middle level students arrive in grade 6 with the basic foundation necessary to organize, study, and become self-directed learners compatible with their developmental level. The middle school focus would be on organization, study skills, note-taking skills, time management, and self-discipline. Academic assignments that are based on the characteristics of young adolescents evidence an enrichment philosophy that allows choice, alternatives, and creativity rather than solely textbook oriented exercises. Middle school assignments would reflect team planning and development. Teams of teachers would collaborate in helping students become more self-directed and self-disciplined.

The guidelines might suggest that while the high school plan would be based upon departments it would reflect that grade-level and team teachers had worked together to ensure that everyone was operating with the students' best interest in mind. The high school planning committee would develop a system to ensure that the skills acquired in the elementary and middle schools were continually being reinforced and that teachers continued to work under John Dewey's philosophy of educating the whole child. Ideally, high school teachers would cooperate so that their students would not be bombarded by several unrelated homework requirements each night.

STEP 6.   Evaluate the overall effectiveness of the homework improvement effort and report the results. The HAT must continually collect, interpret, and report data regarding the extent to which the system-wide homework plan is being implemented. Effective techniques being employed by individual schools can also be shared throughout the system.

For a system-wide homework plan to work, teachers, administrators, and parents must all be involved from the onset. All too often, committees working alone spend considerable time developing a policy which becomes a manual that is largely ignored. Homework can be truly beneficial if a system makes a serious commitment to helping students learn how to study and become independent learners. If teachers do not work together for the benefit of students, the philosophy begins to falter. That is why it is imperative that the teaming strand be evident throughout the entire plan, grades K-12.

AN INDIVIDUAL MIDDLE SCHOOL HOMEWORK PLAN

Once the system has developed a general and flexible homework plan, teachers in individual schools can address the specifics. Each school should work to maintain consistency with the system-wide philosophy. The following steps provide a framework for individual school development of a homework plan:

1. Appoint a Homework Improvement Team (HIT).

2. Review the results of the system-wide HAT's data collection.

3. Identify aspects of the HAT's data collection that pertain to their school.

4. Develop a school-wide homework plan.

5. Work with teams and teachers to implement the plan.

6. Conduct workshops for parents on helping their children become self-directed learners.

7. Oversee homework hotlines, homework clubs, incentive programs, and other activities applicable to the philosophy of the homework plan.

8. Evaluate the effectiveness of the homework improvement effort and report the results to the faculty.

These eight steps are elaborated on in the following paragraphs.

STEP 1. Appoint a Homework Improvement Team (HIT). Some individuals that served on the system-wide committee should be included on the school HIT. Interested parents, students, and teachers are also invited to serve on the committee. The purpose of the committee is to develop a plan and oversee its implementation. The committee should be a working group, committed to making homework a meaningful component of the total curriculum.

STEP 2. Review the results of the HAT's data collection. Through a study of the data collected system-wide, the HIT becomes familiar with the homework problems and policies presently in existence.

STEP 3. Identify aspects of the HAT's data collection that pertain to their school. The HIT assesses those responses from parents, teachers, students, and administrators that represent their school. They also review the data available which summarizes their students' backgrounds, environments, and academic history. The assessment information is used to brainstorm ideas or recommendations for developing the individual school homework plan.

STEP 4. Develop a school-wide homework plan. The school guidelines, while flexible enough to allow teams of teachers to decide on specifics, should be consistent with the system-wide plan. Some decisions may specify that homework in the respective middle school will be: clearly stated as to purpose, relevant, planned by teams, graded punctually, and returned to students for discussion.   The plan also includes the sequence of skills that must be reinforced at each grade level. The HIT can include additional skills if applicable.

STEP 5. Work with teams to implement the plan. The HIT serves as a resource for teams as they instigate homework assignments reflecting the new plan. Areas needing clarification are addressed by the HIT, but most decisions should be determined by the teams.

STEP 6. Conduct workshops for parents on helping their children at home. The HIT works with parents in providing study skills and time management workshops so they can assist their children in developing self-discipline. Workshops should be ongoing throughout the year and repeated for new parents as needed.

STEP 7. Oversee homework hotlines, homework clubs, incentive programs and other activities applicable to the philosophy of the local plan. The HIT determines the school-wide efforts to emphasize the importance of homework and its proper use. If a homework hotline is to be used, the committee can investigate means of making this service available. Many business partners happily share their phone lines with schools after business hours. Individual team homework assignments and other related school information is recorded daily and available to the public through the hotline number.

If the HIT decides to include a school-wide detention program related to homework, the best way to implement the program can be developed. A school in Pennsylvania implemented a policy which stated that when students miss three homework assignments during a grading period, they are immediately assigned to after-school detention. The administrator reports that homework completion has increased as a result of this policy. Care must be taken, however, not to develop negative attitudes about homework by emphasizing compliance alone.

The HIT also investigates the possibility of implementing homework clubs, school-wide incentive programs, and other activities to show students the importance of homework. Alternatives for students without home support must be a major consideration of the school-wide program.

STEP 8. Evaluate the effectiveness of the homework improvement effort and report the results to the faculty. The HIT meets regularly to discuss various practices being used and reviews the advantages and disadvantages of the plan. Teachers are given a forum to discuss activities that are successful and involve students. If the system and school have made a commitment to homework then it is worth the effort and time to address all components.

TEAM PLANNING

The system-wide Homework Advisory Team assessed the total system, then broke down the skills and determined a basic sequence of development. Through the system-wide plan, students entering the 6th grade would have been introduced to and had work with study skills, organizational skills, time management skills, and other skills as determined by the HAT.

Each school's Homework Improvement Team (HIT) developed a school-wide philosophy compatible with the system's plan. HIT is also responsible for continually evaluating the effectiveness of homework in the school. This committee also gives each team a list of sequential skills that students will work on and refine in each grade (note-taking, study skills, etc.). A school-wide commitment has been made to help students learn how to become organized through notebooks, calendars, and assignment sheets that everyone will use.

Now the most important part of the plan must occur — the planning by the teaching team. Major decisions are made at this level. For any plan to be effective it (1) must have a system-wide commitment, (2) must be supported consistently by each school, and most importantly, (3) must have team support and follow-through at the school and team level. Teams must work with other grade level and school-wide teams to ensure schoolwide consistency. Ideally, all exploratory and elective teachers are assigned to teams and will be major contributors. The following steps are recommended for developing an individual team homework plan.

1. Review the system-wide and school-wide plans and philosophies so that all team decisions are in concert with established guidelines.

2. Plan a team meeting to focus specifically on homework.

3. Develop a team newsletter explaining the role of homework.

4. Plan a team assembly to explain the year's expectations, emphasizing organizational skills and team collaboration.

5. Maintain homework as an ongoing agenda item for team meetings.

6. Work with the school-wide homework committee to inform them of successful experiences and related team decisions.

7. Evaluate the effectiveness of the team plan and students' involvement on a continual basis.

These seven steps are described in detail below.

STEP 1. **Review the system-wide and school-wide plans and philosophies, so that all team decisions are in concert with established guidelines.** The team then decides on its purposes for homework and its plans regarding nature and frequency of assignments.

STEP 2. **Plan a team meeting to focus specifically on homework.** A list of topics to be discussed should be generated to determine ways the team will operate. Suggested topics for team discussion and decisions include the following ten areas.

(1) TEAM PHILOSOPHY.

The philosophy should reflect the school and system-wide plans, of course. But it should also speak directly to the particular team's view of its objectives and how homework relates to those goals.

(2) FREQUENCY AND AMOUNT OF HOMEWORK.

A plan to ensure that students are not overloaded with assignments or major projects on any given night or week needs to be developed. The team also should determine an *approximate* amount of time needed to complete assignments in each subject per night. Teams can further discuss how tests and quizzes will be scheduled and ways to work together in helping students organize their notebooks and maintain assignment books. The goal is to avoid giving students several different sets of expectations and requirements.

Days when homework will be assigned and whether it will be given on weekends and holidays should be determined.

(3) EVALUATION AND GRADING OF HOMEWORK.

If assignments are important enough to give they should be important enough to evaluate. Different means of evaluation should be discussed and agreement reached on how assignments will be reviewed and recognized. Procedures could include students evaluating their own papers, cooperative learning groups discussing one another's work and even completing one "perfect paper" for the group, pairs working together, and/or teacher evaluation. The practice of students exchanging and correcting one another's papers is not always the best practice. It can embarrass students who do not understand the material in the assignment, but it also has value under certain conditions.

The team should discuss how much homework will count toward the final grade. Consistency among team members is important. Counting homework as 25% of the final grade seemed to be a general recommendation of respondents to the survey.

(4) CONSEQUENCES FOR NOT COMPLETING HOMEWORK.

Teams need to agree on procedures for dealing with students who do not complete assignments. Is the behavior prevalent in all classes? If just one class, that teacher should re-evaluate the assignments being given and work with other team members to determine what they are doing to assist students in completing assignments. If a student is having difficulty in all areas, the team may want to schedule a meeting with the student and parents. Other consequences that might be considered include: (a) missing free time, (b) before or after school detention, (c) assignment to a monitored homework or study group, or (d) depriving the student of other team privileges.

In Hawaii, Castle High School has established a "lunch bunch" policy for students not completing homework assignments. The school believes the policy has sent a message to students in the school that homework IS important and WILL be completed. The letter sent to parents explaining the policy follows.

Dear Parents:

Class assignments and homework are a student's investment in his or her education. It not only provides the teacher with necessary feedback, but also provides the students with the opportunity to demonstrate the skills and knowledge he or she has acquired. Assignments are an essential part of the learning process. It is therefore essential that all assignments be completed in a timely manner.

When students do not complete or turn in assignments, we will ask them to come in to guided study sessions. It is our hope that the additional time and motivation will allow them to complete their assignments. It is also our hope that parents will support us in this effort.

Guided study will be held daily immediately following period 4. This is the time that students would normally be going to lunch. We plan to have students escorted to Rm. 23 where they will be monitored by Mr. Kane. Lunch will be brought in for anyone so desiring it. Students will remain in Rm 23 until they have completed their assignments or until lunch recess ends.

We understand the imposition we are making on our students' "free time," but we hope you can see the high priority assignment completion must have for all our students. We have not utilized after-school time for guided study as this time has been earmarked for tutorial purposes.

Again we hope all students will be responsible for completing all assignments. If they are not, we hope that you as parents will be supportive of our efforts to get them back on task.

Sincerely,

Castle Gold Core Teachers
Castle High School, Hawaii

(5) TYPES OF HOMEWORK ASSIGNMENTS.

Teams should discuss more imaginative and relevant assignments keeping in mind the characteristics of students, the purposes of homework, options, creativity, thinking skills, and the four levels recommended by Lee and Pruitt (*practice, preparation, extension, and creativity*). Team members might want to agree to complete one another's homework assignments occasionally to obtain a better understanding of what they are requiring students to do as well as the time commitment required. Different types of assignments are addressed in Chapter 6.

(6) WAYS TO INVOLVE PARENTS AND GUARDIANS.

The team should communicate to parents/guardians some ways they can help their children with homework. In addition to the usual suggestions about a quiet place and regular schedule consider ways that parents can play an active role in homework rather than just a supervisory role. (Step 3, p. 51 gives additional details)

(7) INCENTIVES.

Different types of incentives can be used on occasion to encourage completion of homework. Students should not receive an incentive every time they complete an assignment, however. Some suggestions include:

(a) homework breaks — give students a night off

(b) homework coupons — used at student's discretion to get one night with no homework and used in any one of the team's classes

(c) free time — a class period or portion of it which can be used for discussions, listening to a favorite radio station, or other student-selected activity

(d) positive notes home

(e) praise — low-key so the student is not embarrassed

(f) homework heroes/heroines — recognize students who have completed their homework by giving them a special treat or lunch with the principal

(g) homework lottery — students completing their assignments add their name to a jar and once a week 4-5 names are drawn to receive a special incentive determined by the team

(h) class competitions — classes compete against one another. The class in which all students turn in their homework for a predesignated number of days wins a special treat (see Chapter 6)

(i) double grades — students receive credit in two subjects for one assignment that grows out of an interdisciplinary approach.

(8) ALTERNATIVES.

Teams should be ready to deal with students that do not have the environment, support, or materials to accomplish homework assignments. Alternatives might include a homework "club" where students work under supervision in the school, a special time established in the morning or afternoon when a team member can work with students, or individualized contracts.

(9) INTERDISCIPLINARY ASSIGNMENTS.

Homework can be an excellent way of implementing the interdisciplinary approach. Teams should continually work to integrate their assignments. For instance, if students are studying measurement in math and paragraph structure in language arts, the homework assignment would call for them to measure some things at home and write a paragraph describing their properties, size, etc. The assignment would receive credit in both classes.

(10) MISSED HOMEWORK DUE TO ABSENCES.

A plan to work with students that are regularly absent is needed. Maintaining an ongoing assignment book or section of bulletin board that students can check when they miss a day is one aid. Also, cooperative groups should be responsible for informing their members of activities and assignments missed.

STEP 3. Develop a team newsletter and letter to parents explaining the team philosophy, homework requirements and procedures, grading system, and an overview of the years' activities. Sent to every student's parent/guardian, the communications can be an effective means of establishing positive connections to the home.

Parents should be encouraged to "assist" their children but not complete assignments for them. An administrator wrote, "Home assignments are not just paper and pencil exercises. We should spend equal amounts of time explaining home assignments to parents and their role in them."

Ways to get parents involved through workshops and open houses need to be considered. A teacher from Toronto, Ontario wrote, "Our school/community consists of a large number of multi-racial, multi-ethnic groups who are also working class. Parents, for the most part, trust that the school will educate their child and do not participate on a regular basis. There is no Parent-Teacher Association in the school. Parents oftentimes do not attend school events due to busy work schedules. As teachers, we feel parents in our community want homework but cannot support its completion at home. This may be because families have other priorities. Those students who do well on homework and do it regularly are those whose parents make it known that school work is valued and reinforce the process consistently. As teachers, we have not given up. We have designed a parent workshop on homework which was very successful last winter. This year we will give the workshop early in the year. The Grade 7 Team goal for this year has been to develop organization and responsibility through homework."

STEP 4. Plan a team assembly to explain the year ahead emphasizing organizational skills and team collaboration. Talk about the importance of homework and let students know the basic decisions the team of teachers has made such as "no homework on weekends and holidays." Develop team mottos and slogans encouraging homework, i.e. "Homework is a HIT on the Seminole Team." Invite parents to attend the assembly.

Garvin (1990) explained how one team met every Monday to discuss homework assignments. All team members agreed to write the team's weekly assignments on their chalkboards so students could keep track of their assignments from class to class and know that the teachers were aware of one another's assignments.

STEP 5. Make homework an ongoing agenda item. Team members should discuss and coordinate assignments regularly. Teams should work together to reinforce the consistency of assignments and emphasize the importance of time management.

Teams will find many good suggestions in *20 Successful Homework Strategies — Tried, Tested, and Proven* prepared by the Institute for Educational Research (*Teacher Today* series, 793 North Main, Glen Ellyn, Illinois, 60137, 708-858-8060): It includes the following:

1) Assign homework only when you feel the assignment is valuable. A night off is better than homework which serves no worthwhile purpose.
2) Allow sufficient time to fully explain each assignment. Tell students:
   - the assignment at the beginning of the lesson to be sure you have enough time for a thorough explanation.
   - the purpose of the assignment (e.g., to increase understanding of two figures of speech, metaphors and alliteration),
   - what specific outcome should result (e.g., a paragraph comparing two poets' styles).
3) Give the specifics — the due date, format and special materials needed.
4) Present the assignment verbally and in writing. Choose a consistent, highly visible location to display homework assignments each day.
5) Ask a different student each day to repeat the directions for the assignment to the class.
6) Require students to record assignments in a notebook.
7) Explain your procedures for makeup and late assignments. Tell students what the consequences are for failure to turn in assignments and for late homework.
8) Communicate homework procedures and consequences to parents at the beginning of the school year and later as needed.

9) Clarify assignments when students seem unsure of what to do:
- give examples of similar tasks that the class has done before. These may also be similar tasks from a different subject area.
- read and display examples of the finished product completed by students last year.
- demonstrate how the task or subtask is to be done. This is particularly helpful if you repeat the mental steps to go through while performing the task.

10) Give assignments that are designed for students to do well on independently. Research shows that achievement increases when success rates are high (90 to 100%).

11) Avoid assignments that require adult help as that may put some students at a disadvantage.

12) Plan your homework assignments for an entire week and present students with the schedules a week in advance.

13) Provide an outline of long-term projects well in advance of due dates.

14) Outline and order subtasks which students must do to successfully complete a complex assignment. If necessary, set deadlines for completion of each subtask and evaluate student progress.

15) Make sure that outside resources necessary to completing an assignment are readily available to all students.

16) Provide alternative ways for students with skill deficiencies to complete assignments:
- use volunteers to tape-record textbook chapters.
- allow students who have difficulty writing to dictate information to a parent, another adult or older sibling or friend.

17) Make allowances for students who are unable to work at the pace of their peers:
- designate the amount of time that they are expected to spend on a given assignment.
- accept the amount of work completed during that time. A parent's signature can verify the time spent.

18) Give assignments only for instructional purposes, not as punishment.

19) Design a form for students to log the time they spend each day on homework in each subject. This will give them:
- a realistic picture of how many minutes they are spending on assignments, and
- the connection between the time they spend and the grades they earn.

20) Have students pick a homework "buddy." They can exchange phone numbers, explain an assignment and help with solutions to a problem. Emphasize to the class that just giving a buddy the answer doesn't help the classmate learn.

STEP 6. **Inform the school-wide committee of successful activities and experiences.** Let the committee know if a breakdown in the system-wide philosophy begins to occur, i.e. students lacking simple organizational skills upon entering the middle school.

STEP 7. **Evaluate continuously the effectiveness of the team plan.** Determine if alternatives are needed to assist students with their homework. Look into the possibility of establishing homework clubs, homework hotlines, and cross-age tutoring groups to work with other grades.

EXAMPLES OF HOMEWORK POLICIES

The following examples are policies currently operational in these schools.

In Owen Brown Middle School, Columbia, Maryland, a daily assignment sheet is employed and the homework policy is printed in the handbook. Included there are the following tips to parents provided by Principal Marion Payne.

Remember:
Home assignments are your child's responsibility — not yours. However, they do need your encouragement and support. Specifically, your child needs consistency in when, where, and how they should complete their home assignments. Following are some simple suggestions as to how you can be the most effective support when it's homework time.

• **Area**
Provide a quiet, well-lit area for your child to do his/her home assignment. This area should feel comfortable and always be available at homework time.

• Tools

Provide "tools" for doing home assignments: pencil, pen, paper, dictionary (very inexpensive paperback ones can be obtained at drug stores, book stores, or department stores.) A desk or table-top makes the best place to do homework (not the knees, lap, or floor).

• Adapt Learning Style

Observe your child's learning style and adapt homework time accordingly, i.e. some students would rather have some leisure time directly after a long day at school — so just before or after dinner would be preferable. Some students would rather complete their homework after just arriving home from school.

Whatever is best for your child is okay, but be consistent.

• Proofread

Help your child proofread work but errors should be corrected by the student.

• Calendar

Keep a calendar close by and, along with your child, mark important "due dates" so that unexpected or unpleasant home assignment "surprises" can be avoided.

• Homework

If your child consistently tells you that he or she has no homework, make further inquiries. Chances are, he/she is hedging.

• Be Positive!

Be positive, show approval. Your child needs and wants your caring self.

The Desert View Middle School in El Paso, Texas has a homework program that has been quite successful. Principal Nick Pike provided the following description of their program.

Desert View Middle School has several student organizational and study skills programs in effect that work extremely well to limit homework assignments to students and help them to complete successfully the assignments given.

A Desert View Academic Team consists of a math, science, English, and social studies teacher. One special education teacher and a health or computer education teacher meet at least once a week with the academic team. The team has a common preparation time each day, and each day they have specific tasks to perform. On Tuesday of each week during the school year, the team must coordinate all homework and extra assignments for the next five school days. They may make assignments in any way they find to be most appropriate for student success; however, assignments given by the team teachers should not take more than one hour and thirty minutes to perform. Each teacher in the team is also asked to complete homework assignments that the other members of the team assign to students. Group discussions of this event help to insure time regulations and proper difficulty for the students.

Three ring binders, subject dividers, pens, and #2 pencils are required of every student for every subject during the day. If, for whatever reason, a student does not have the three ring binder, he is not allowed into class. That student is sent to the office where he receives a "loaner" three ring binder to use for the day.

The three ring binders each have assignment books included and each teacher has the students write the class objective and any assignment in the assignment book. This allows the teacher, student, and parents to work collectively to enhance organizational skills needed to insure student success.

The Parent Handbook at Shrewsbury Middle School, Shrewsbury, Massachusetts, includes the following statements that were provided by Principal Preston Shaw.

Middle School Homework Policy

Homework is a major component and a vital part of the Middle School program. It is an extension of the regular daily school program and, as such, it ought to have the same thoughtful, creative consideration and planning given to other aspects of the program. The goal is to help students develop good homework/study habits through regular homework assignments.

Purpose of Homework Assignments

Homework assignments should generally fulfill one or more of the following purposes.

1. Drill and additional practice to reinforce and/or strengthen skills introduced in the classroom.

2. Guided reading of assigned literature or text materials.

3. Research activities in locating information.

4. Work on reports or projects of a long-term nature.

Long-Range Assignments

Long range homework assignments can provide valuable learning experiences for middle school students. Assignments such as book reports, research projects, science projects, models, and collections take careful planning on the part of the teacher and good organization on the part of the student. With such assignments, keep in mind:

1. A long-range assignment ought to be viewed as a series of shorter assignments which call for periodic checking by the teacher.

2. A long-range assignment ought not exceed a period of more than four weeks.

3. There needs to be specific written directions for the student including purpose, expectations, procedures to be used, and due dates.

4. Students should not be faced with several, unrelated long-range assignments at one time.

Amount of Homework

The amount of homework assigned normally increases as the student progresses through school. While it is not feasible to establish rigid time limits, the following guidelines were suggested for students in one school:

grade 5   30 minutes minimum to 60 minutes maximum
grade 6   30 minutes minimum to 75 minutes maximum
grade 7   45 minutes minimum to 90 minutes maximum

The minutes represent recommended time to be spent on homework for all subjects combined.

Late Homework

It is the student's responsibility to see that homework assignments are handed in or are ready to be checked on the due date assigned by the teacher. Homework assignments not ready on the date due will be accepted on the following day if accompanied by a parent's note. An assignment will not be accepted beyond that day and the student will receive a zero for that assignment.

It is not the responsibility of an individual teacher or the teaching team to provide parents and students with a list of missing assignments during or at the end of a term. Homework is, most often, an immediate need that reinforces a skill learned that day or prepares students for the next day's lesson. To make up assignments days or weeks later serves little or no purpose.

Requests for extensions on long-range assignments will be given upon parental requests prior to the date due.

Weekend-Vacation Assignments

It is preferable that homework not be assigned to be done on week-ends, however, there may be certain times and certain assignments when a week-end is the best time for an assignment to be done. In any event, efforts should be made to keep week-end homework assignments restricted.

Homework Requests Due to Absences

When students are absent from school it is their responsibility to get assignments made up upon their return. It is strongly suggested that the student contact another student in class to cover one or two day absences. This "buddy system" has proved to work quite well. If this cannot be done, the student is encouraged to stay after school for extra help. Teachers are available for extra help every Monday through Thursday.

Parent calls for homework are to be honored on the third consecutive day that a student is absent. The parent should

a. contact the school prior to 11:00 a.m.
b. tell the secretary the student's team, locker number and combination, and what books the child has at home.

The secretary will fill out a homework request form so that the teachers can get it during the lunch period.

The requested assignments are to be left in the main office at the close of school and can be picked up after 2:45 p.m.

Parents should understand that it is a time consuming task for a team to fill out and circulate a homework request sheet for a student. On any given day there may be several students absent. It should also be noted that since homework is often based on a lesson taught that day, that work for absentees requires a different approach. It is therefore, more effective for students absent one or two days to stay after school for the extra help session.

Parent Help: All students are to use a homework assignment book. Parents should check this assignment book on a regular basis in order for this to be an effective tool.

Parents are responsible for setting guidelines for good study habits at home. They should monitor the time allotment for homework and see that there is no interruption from television, radio or stereo.

SUMMARY

Does it sound like a great deal of work to practice the recommendations made in this chapter? Yes! For homework to be effective, the necessary preliminary and sequential components must be evident. Arbitrarily assigning homework with no planning, collaboration, or follow-up is usually a futile effort. In essence, teachers must remember that to be effective they must also be team players, supporting and reinforcing the decisions that have been made at all levels. If homework is important then it should be planned for and sequentially reinforced throughout the entire system. Most importantly, it should not be assigned just because of tradition — assign homework for a valid educational purpose. Make assignments exciting and different. Be creative and do not develop a plan just because someone stated "effective schools give homework." Remember, we are closing in on a new century — isn't it time we began thinking in a new way with a new direction concerning all educational practices including homework?

6. Can homework really be innovative?

Is "innovative homework" an oxymoron? In all too many cases it is, because many teachers don't take the time to plan meaningful assignments or evaluate sufficiently the purpose and effectiveness of their assignments. WHAT is assigned for homework and HOW it is evaluated make all the difference. To be fully effective, homework assignments must incorporate some student choice, variety, and encourage creativity.

The most beneficial assignments are collaboratively planned by teachers and are based on the known characteristics of early adolescents. Laura M. Robertson stated,

> Before educators can help to eliminate some of the stresses our young people are feeling, it is necessary to peer into the hearts, minds, and bodies of middle school children. Like flowers waiting to bloom, they are planted in our gardens. If we love, nurture, and feed them, they will blossom into beautiful individuals. If we loathe and neglect their uniqueness, we pluck away their self-esteem — one petal at a time.

Lest we unintentionally pluck petals, it is vital for educators to develop homework assignments that are compatible with the characteristics of young adolescent students.

ASSIGNMENTS BASED ON STUDENTS'
PHYSICAL AND MENTAL CHARACTERISTICS

Physically, early adolescents are constantly changing and growing. They need to be active, putting to use their endless supply of energy. Assignments that get them into the community or walking through a mall to gather data are more exciting than ones which have them sitting alone completing "busywork."

Allowing students to experiment with their own individual learning styles is effective. Ask them to complete an assignment one night in complete silence sitting upright, the next night with the radio and/or television in the background, and the next night comfortably sprawled on the floor. Students should keep a diary of the different conditions under which they completed their assignments and how they felt about the effect of the context on the quality of their homework and their feelings toward completing it.

Advocate nutritional snacks while completing assignments and have students keep track of what they eat and drink while working on homework. They can write the information in their homework diaries or in the corner of the paper.

Students learn when they are having fun. As one teacher stated, "Homework can be great enrichment. Homework can also be used to read over material, thus saving class time for discussion. What homework isn't — often enough — is FUN. It is too bad that we miss opportunities to make learning exciting!"

Invite students to master facts or vocabulary words through the use of self-composed raps and movement. A cheerleader recently explained that she remembered information for tests by using her cheering motions when searching for the answer. Encouraging mnemonic devices and techniques also may unlock many creative doors while allowing the competitive spirit in students to unfold.

ASSIGNMENTS BASED ON STUDENTS'
INTELLECTUAL CHARACTERISTICS

Provide assignments that will involve students in ways other than completing a ditto or copying something from a reference book. Early adolescents prefer active learning; assignments should involve several of their senses and provide for some choice. The short attention span of early adolescents and their learning styles are other considerations.

Teach students how to break the tasks into segments so they have time to think about what they are doing. Encourage them to keep track of the amount of time they spend on specific tasks in their homework diaries or at the top of their paper. Students should write the time they started the assignment and every break taken until the time of completion. The completion time should also be documented. Teams should take time to analyze these time studies and discuss the results with students.

Young adolescents enjoy learning things they consider to be useful and related to real-life problems. As stated by Buzan (1984) the power of the brain is immense. Students need to be encouraged to use their minds to the fullest extent. Assignments should be structured so students not only enjoy doing them but also see their relevance. Determining the caloric intake of a meal is an activity girls especially enjoy while determining the number of miles from one location to another by alternate routes is usually enjoyed by boys. Interviewing a community or family member to find out more about the community or past events is an effective assignment.

We know how curious students are at this age so we should give them assignments that capitalize on this trait. Many activities can be based on the newspaper, discovering political issues, analyzing ads, interpreting cartoons, finding new words, etc. Television is also an excellent resource that can be exploited positively as a basis for homework assignments.

Futuristic-type activities which invite students to look into the next century and devise a plan of technology or invent a necessary device also excite students. Activities that elicit creative thinking prove to be much more successful than basic drill and practice.

Fantasy is another valuable angle to employ in assigning homework. In any subject you can have students fantasize about a situation that occurred after school dealing with a topic in school. Most students love to share their fantasies.

ASSIGNMENTS BASED ON STUDENTS'
SOCIAL CHARACTERISTICS

Recognizing the social needs of these students, teachers should encourage students to work on homework assignments in pairs or small groups on occasion. One school had students set up a "phonework" system in which students spent a certain amount of time on the phone calling one another and checking answers. This should not be done too often since parents might get upset because of tied-up lines, but it is a fun way to get students working together.

Incorporate heroes and heroines into their homework. Students look to these role models for fashion and behavior and we should let them introduce us to their heroes. Teachers learn much about students when they see who they look up to. Reading about their heroes, writing about their lives, looking into their backgrounds and birthplaces, and their talents are all topics that could be incorporated into many subjects and assignments.

Activities that involve students in community-related and assistance roles helps show them the necessity of being respectful and courteous. Assignments that encourage work at a nearby hospital or nursing home many times give students a new outlook on life. Even an assignment of "just do something nice for someone in your life tonight" can reap many benefits.

Assignments in which students have to teach a lesson and become the teacher for a class or small group or even their parents also open many eyes. Students then realize the "homework" teachers do every night in preparation for teaching and get a better understanding of the demands of teaching.

Reversal assignments in which students must go one night without the use of any electrical appliances or the telephone sometimes gives them an appreciation for our world. Such activities always bring about insightful discussions.

Identify the important possessions in the lives of early adolescents and tie them into homework assignments. Girls at this age enjoy reading teen magazines to keep current on fashion and fads. Design assignments that will allow students to use magazines to discover types of products available or propaganda techniques employed by advertisers. Boys also have favorite magazines on sports or motorcycles that can be used in some homework assignments.

Most students, particularly girls, love to pass notes. Use this favorite pastime as a basis for a homework assignment in which students must write a note to a peer explaining the chapter they just read (allow them to express true opinions) or are about to read. Ask students to write a note to another class or the teacher summarizing the material read. This type of activity allows students to state their opinions freely.

Early adolescents love competition so we should provide positive competitive experiences. A Virginia teacher mounted a paper football field with yardage markers on a bulletin board. Each math class has a football taped to the field. Whenever an entire class completes the homework assignments their football is moved ten yards down the field toward the goal. The class that reaches the goal line first wins one math period to play math games. This activity gets all classes involved and has worked successfully.

ASSIGNMENTS BASED ON THE
EMOTIONAL CHARACTERISTICS

Early adolescents have a tendency to be moody (understatement of the year). Opportunities to express their feelings and identify their moods can reveal so much. An interesting assignment is to have students document their different moods while completing homework assignments. Students can document their feelings in homework diaries or draw faces depicting their mood and write a short rationale on the margin of their paper. This "mood check" can give teachers an opportunity to understand the feelings students have during homework. Different moods may explain reasons for sloppy papers or incomplete responses.

Another activity that involves emotions is to ask students to openly evaluate homework assignments upon completion. They can write somewhere on their homework paper what they liked/disliked and what they understood or did not comprehend. Students then are allowed to discuss their feelings during class time without being penalized. Most students are good evaluators of teachers and the best teachers listen carefully to what their students say.

To determine reasons for incomplete or unsubmitted assignments the following technique is effective. When collecting homework assignments require *everyone* to pass in a paper. Students not completing the assignment *must* turn in a paper with their name and date and a detailed justification for no assignment. Their explanation must address *why* they do not have their assignment and *what* they would do if they were the teacher. One student required to explain his reasons in writing for no homework stated to his teacher, "Forget it, it would have been easier to do the assignment than write the reason for not having it — I will not forget tonight!"

Keeping in mind the emotional needs of students, homework assignments ought to sanction choices. Allow students to develop creative homework assignments on their own using a variety of resources and occasionally working together. A teacher in Georgia allows her students to create their own school, to develop laws to govern the school, and to describe what a town would be like if no one worked as well as other hypothetical situations.

INNOVATIVE ASSIGNMENTS

Every assignment that a teacher or team sends home is a public relations message. The assignment gives parents an idea of what is being studied in the classroom and an indication of their child's reaction to each subject and teacher. Consequently, planning for homework is *as important as preparing classroom lessons.* Too often, homework is given simply because that is the way it has always been. We continue to base decisions on our own educational experiences forgetting today's society and students.

Using students to plan homework can be interesting. A recent observation demonstrated that middle level students can be creative and do complete assignments when they are involved in the decisions. A teacher was planning a unit on the Sahara. He asked the students for suggestions for culminating projects. They gave several suggestions that included role-playing as a travel agent advertising the Sahara, designing a mobile, designing a diorama, and preparing a video presentation. After all of the students were allowed to brainstorm suggestions, the teacher informed them of due dates, explained how a work corner would be set up to help them get started, and emphasized the fact that they could work in groups. He further encouraged them to be as creative as possible. The teacher reminded students of their homework and the due date. Very little time was allotted during class to work on the assignments due to time constraints. On the day of the final projects, every student had something and participated in a formal presentation. The projects ranged from a simple written report to a video presentation, yet they were all unique and students were proud. Most importantly, it was evident that the students had fun and actually had learned something about the Sahara.

Homework does not have to be an "enemy" or take up an entire evening. It can be relevant and provide diversity. Students are more likely to internalize information when they are involved. As one teacher stated, "To recall information that has been discussed or presented in class sessions is a vital part of students' learning but should not be the only way. If it is, students learn the *fill-n-flush* method of recall where they fill their minds by short-term memorization of facts, and immediately flush the information after a test."

We all can relate to that reality, especially when we ask students a question about information discussed the previous month and they look at us as though we are from another planet. Thus, another reason for carefully planned assignments is to engage students sufficiently in their learning while they are processing the information. A useful tool to assist in planning such homework assignments is Bloom's *Taxonomy*.

The taxonomy is a valuable tool which can suggest ways that students can explore subjects. It also gives teachers the opportunity to develop a thinking curriculum in which students must think about their level of understanding and apply skills creatively. Schurr (1989) presented in *Dynamite in the Classroom* excellent examples of classroom activities at each level of the taxonomy. An extension of classroom activities used for homework on the topic of propaganda, for instance, may include :

Knowledge Level Assignments

a . List all the different types of media available for advertising.

b. Design a poster showing different forms of propaganda used in advertising.

Comprehension Level Assignments

a. Cut out pictures of different types of propaganda techniques used in magazines and translate their meaning.

b. Describe a product using the "emotional words" technique.

Application Level Assignments

a. Develop a campaign strategy using the "bandwagon" technique.

b. Prepare a rationale for using a good friend in a "testimonial" advertisement.

Analysis Level Assignments

a. After viewing commercials on television, classify the techniques used for your favorite products.

b. Compare and contrast the different propaganda techniques in a creative way.

Synthesis Level Assignments

a. Design an advertisement campaign using one of the propaganda techniques.

b. Invent something that would help students in school and develop a commercial introducing the product.

Evaluation Level Assignments

a. Provide examples of four propaganda techniques and evaluate the effectiveness of each.

b. Develop an advertisement for a nonexistent product and survey your friends and family to see if they would purchase the product.

Activities that involve the taxonomy lead students into critical thinking. These activities force students to move beyond the knowledge and application levels where most of our learning and instruction occurs.

Additional activities, based on Lee and Pruitt's four levels, help teachers begin to think creatively about assignments. Remember, the best assignments emphasize choice and variety, and are related to the developmental needs of young adolescents. The following are examples of possible assignments in the four levels:

Practice Assignments

- Compose five sentences summarizing the information discussed in class today. (any subject)

- Develop five word problems and solve each one. The problems will be given to classmates. (math)

- Write a paragraph or two describing your activities after school today. Then write a paragraph about what you wish you could do tomorrow after school. (language arts)

- Listen to the weather report tonight and summarize in writing what the prevailing conditions are and what to expect tomorrow. (science and language arts)

- Interview a senior citizen to tap his or her memories of the great depression. Prepare a written report containing at least five main points. (social studies and language arts)

Preparation Assignments

- Design five questions that could be asked on a test covering the information you read tonight. (any subject)

- Reviewing only the pictures and charts in the chapter, prepare an overview of what you think the chapter will entail based on the illustrations. (any subject)

- Locate six to eight different sized canned foods in your home and write down the number of ounces contained in each can. (math)

- Find two articles in the newspaper — one containing factual information and one containing opinion. Compare and contrast the two pieces. (language arts and social studies)

- Find or draw pictures of animals that you think are carnivorous. (science)

- Ask three people to explain, in their own words, the reason for the Vietnam war. (social studies)

Extension Assignments

- Write in newspaper format, an article describing something that recently occurred in class. Include a headline. (any subject)

- Prepare an ad showing the savings of an item you are selling compared to a similar item being sold by a competitor. (math)

- Take a side concerning the death penalty and present some supporting arguments. (social studies and language arts)

- Design a brochure that explains the effects of pollution and give ways to avoid it. (science and language arts)

- Write a descriptive paragraph about your ideal bedroom. (language arts)

- Invent something that might make our lives easier. Describe it. (science/language arts)

Creative Assignments

- Write your own version of the chapter just completed in our text. (any subject)

- Create an autobiography using only pictures. (social studies/language arts)

- Design and describe the perfect school — what would you study, what activities would you engage in, and even what would you eat? (any subject)

- Prepare a project that demonstrates something you have learned as a result of the unit. (any subject)

- Design a low calorie menu for a week. (science/health)

- Pretend you are running for a particular public office — develop a campaign slogan, speech, and platform. (social studies/language arts)

- Design a commercial to convince students of the importance of the concept(s) being studied. (any subject)

- Create a play or television show, using humor as the central focus. (language arts)

- Design your own country. Explain the culture, inhabitants, industry, and other features. Include a map, flag, city names, and government structure. (social studies)

- Present a book report in a creative way — video, t-shirt scenes, diorama, mobile, role playing, or other alternative method. (any subject)

All four levels of assignments can be used throughout the middle level years. Each one can provide experiences that will help students become involved in organizing their time, completing assignments, and becoming self-directed learners. Many, such as the "create your own country" suggestion, lend themselves to being a small group assignment. Others can be interdisciplinary in nature.

Citing that old saw, "What is everybody's business is nobody's business," Lounsbury (1989) claimed that "with few exceptions, whenever a single, common assignment is given to a class of middle school students it is a questionable assignment." He goes on to suggest a way to make a typical "read-Chapter-12-for-tomorrow's-discussion" assignment more specific. Have each row of students read the chapter with a very specific but limited purpose. For instance, those in one row might each be expected to prepare a few good test questions covering the chapter while those in another row might identify and be ready to define new or difficult words in the chapter. Those in a third row could each be responsible for developing an outline to be posted and students seated in a fourth row might be ready to provide supplementary information on persons or characters mentioned. Even if a fifth row got the night off, the class discussion the following day would likely be quite productive.

A number of suggestions for assigning resourceful homework assignments to middle level students were developed by Arth and Olson (1980). They set forth nine types of assignments that recognize the unique nature of students. These types are described briefly below.

1. The *parent-student homework* assignment is started in class by the students but must be accomplished at home with the assistance of a parent or guardian. This assignment provides parents and their children with the opportunity to talk about school and become partners in the learning enterprise.

2. *Group homework* requires input from all the students in a class or from a group of students. This assignment requires students to communicate with one other outside of the classroom. Students would investigate a question or problem posed by the class.

3. *Differentiated homework* provides the students with some choice. Given a list of ten problems, students can select out the problems they do not understand and complete only those they comprehend. Students must do some problems, however. This activity allows students to see that it is okay not to know everything.

4. *Roulette homework* allows students to spin a hand on a wheel to determine the number of problems or questions they must complete that night for homework. If two students select the same number, they can work together. Consider writing "no homework" in one of the wheel's sections. Students love to get the night off.

5. *Mix and match homework* allows students to substitute an assignment from another class if they can provide an adequate justification. This helps students understand the integrated nature of the world. Teams could also plan for this type of activity.

6. *Write and tell homework* is a means of assuring that all students understand the assignment. Teachers write the assignment on the board then have students tell one another exactly what to do. Students paraphrase the assignment to a peer to demonstrate understanding.

7. *Television related homework* uses the media to involve students in out-of-class assignments. This assignment has students viewing television with a purpose in mind (propaganda, weather reports, statistics of sports). Since students are engaged in television viewing

throughout the week, teachers can capitalize on a regular early adolescent activity.

8. *Student generated homework* allows students to write questions and prepare assignments for one another. This activity makes students accept more responsibility for their own education.

9. *Teacher-student homework* provides students with the opportunity to see the teacher as a learner. This activity occurs when both the teacher and the student are interested in a subject but do not have the knowledge to discuss it intelligently. The students and teacher are both required to investigate the topic/subject/question and come to class the next day prepared to present new information or opinions on the topic.

While research does not prove one way or another about the effectiveness of homework we do know that students who like their teachers, have pride in their school, and feel respected as human beings will participate in the game of learning. Therefore, it is our job as teachers to do all we can to help students develop positive attitudes toward learning while still permitting them to be early adolescents and enjoy learning. Homework should not be assigned simply because one feels that it is expected. Assign homework so that students will, indeed, learn something and will become more self-disciplined individuals. The greater the intrinsic value of activities the less the need to rely on extrinsic motivators to insure completion.

Many techniques should be used to encourage students into pursuing learning activities after school. Unfortunately, however, there may be those few students that do not think anything related to school is fun or who do not have any home support for educational activities. Such students inevitably have a low self-esteem are not motivated to complete assignments. They lack basic skills and need an extra measure of self-confidence to even attempt certain tasks. Cooperative group assignments can be a valuable technique which provides students with peer support. Other techniques like "study-buddies" and peer tutoring can improve students' motivation and enthusiasm for learning. Teachers should try to make assignments that are engaging and never give up on any student. Assignments should be F.U.N. (fulfilling, uplifting, and nurturing)

"The dog ate my homework"

A middle school dilemma — and a solution

SUSAN J. DAVIS

Teachers at our middle school agreed that homework was valuable and they expected students to do approximately 30 minutes of homework each night. Even after explaining the presumably valid reasons for homework to the students, however, I found many students simply didn't do the assignments. In an attempt to solve the problem, the practice of giving detentions for each unfinished assignment was instituted. That solution overburdened the discipline system, so I began to count homework as part of the final grade. That solution resulted in an increased number of failing grades.

I was frustrated. The public demanded that teachers give more homework but students resisted. One day, I asked some students to tell me why they had not done their assignment. One replied, "The dog ate it!" I knew it was time for action.

A New Plan

After analyzing the problem and the usual solutions, I decided I had been taking too much of the responsibility for education away from the students. Middle school students needed a structured homework plan that would foster self-discipline and make them accountable for the work.

The result of a brainstorming session with several staff members was the **Homework Excuse Sheet,** a form students would fill out whenever they did not complete a homework assignment. The Homework Excuse Sheet consisted of four components. First, an accountability measure for the students was built in. Writing down the reason they did not do the homework might make the students think about the validity of their excuse. Second, the consequences for late papers were clearly stated. Third, the students signed a commitment to finish the work that day. Fourth, a blank for their parent's telephone number was included. If I needed to call a parent about missing work, the information was readily available.

The Homework Excuse Sheets were filed by class for easy access. When discussing students' work with parents, the sheets could be pulled and the parents could be given the stated reasons for missing homework.

Results

The Homework Excuse Sheet worked. After the first quarter's use of the sheet with 140 seventh and eighth grade students, grades dramatically improved; over 60% of my 140 students raised their grades. It worked particularly well for those students who had homework averages below 50%. Since that initial use it has virtually eliminated homework as a factor in causing failing grades.

Conclusion

One of the strongest points of the Homework Excuse Sheet is that it has made the students accountable for their work. They have to provide some rationalization and it becomes the basis for discussion with students and/or parents. Counseling them about rearranging their priorities has more relevance and impact.

With the Homework Excuse Sheet and follow-up counseling my students have become more responsible. Homework no longer goes to the dogs.

Susan Davis is a reading teacher at Cary Junior High School in Cary, Illinois.

WOULD YOU BELIEVE THE DOG ATE IT?
or
THE "I didn't do my homework" EXCUSE SHEET

NAME_____   DATE _____

CLASS _____   PERIOD _____

ASSIGNMENT _____

Why didn't you do the assignment?

_____

_____

_____

I understand that I may turn in this assignment by 2:35 for a late grade (one grade lower than the paper earns). If I have not finished this assignment by 2:35, I will stay after school in room 115 until it is finished. I know I will receive a penalty of two grades if I have to stay after school. If I decide not to do the homework on the day it is due, I know I cannot turn it in late, and that I will get a zero for the assignment. I also realize that Mrs. Davis will call my parents if I am late on three or more homework assignments.

_____
Student's Name

Reprinted from *Middle School Journal* , January 1990

FOR BETTER OR FOR WORSE

FOR BETTER OR FOR WORSE COPYRIGHT 1991 Lynn Johnson.
Reprinted with permission of Universal Press Syndicate.

7. Some final thoughts

The learning opportunities teachers provide both in and out of the classroom influence students' perceptions of school and learning itself. We should not lose sight of this reality. Homework *can* benefit instruction and improve one's perceptions of education if appropriately applied. More commonly, however, it contributes to a negative view of school and learning. Many students do not complete assignments or benefit little from doing so simply because assignments are often meaningless and boring. The resulting disinterest and negative attitude, then, can actually inhibit the learning of students. As the middle school continues its advancement it is clearly time to set a new direction for homework.

When conceptualizing that new direction, educators must recognize the realities of the '90s that effect, directly or indirectly, the traditional use of homework: limited parental support, alienated youth, an increase in the use of drugs, escalating suicide, an epidemic of teenage pregnancies, a curriculum filled to overflowing with information that students see little value in learning, and teachers who feel stressed and anxious. We must assess anew the appropriateness of our curriculum and instructional practices, including homework. We may have lost sight of the main purpose of education — teaching students to "learn how to learn."

Readers of this monograph will have recognized some common strands throughout. One emphasizes the need for school districts to develop a system-wide plan for homework. If students are to be provided with the skills necessary for independent learning they need to experience a sequential system that begins in the early years and builds one grade upon the next.

Second, the many educators who believe homework is important must find the ways to demonstrate to students and their parents that it can contribute to academic achievement. Typical, routine assignments have not been able to demonstrate their effectiveness. Assignments must be planned carefully and provide some *success for all*. Students must be taught how to succeed; they already know how to fail. Homework need not be a device of torture, the focus for a "hassle." Our goal should be for students to find in homework lively, creative, and worthwhile learning experiences.

A third point of emphasis is the need for consistent, progressive skill development. Skills prevail longer than various bits of information and need to be a major focus of every level of education.

Another strand that needs to be highlighted is the need for increased use of an integrated, interdisciplinary approach in the out-of-class assignments. In the years ahead the in-school curriculum is certain to become more integrated and the out-of-school assignments need to reflect this increasing reality.

While homework is a very important and long-standing part of education, so too is the emotional and social development of the young adolescents themselves. We must continue to bring homework practices more in line with the developmental realities of these students. We cannot afford to continue mandating homework based on that old assumption — more homework means increased achievement. The issue is much more complex than that.

HOMEWORK--A NEW DIRECTION!

Homework can be such a drag
To everyone affected!
Especially to the kids who say
"It's boring and never corrected!"

Teachers hate the hassle,
and you often hear them nag,
"What do you mean you've done your homework,
but can't find it in your bag?"

Parents don't look forward
to long hours of stress and tears
and think it takes important time
away from growing years.

So if most teachers, parents, and students
all think homework is a pain,
Why it is so often assigned?
The answer is quite plain.

There's a group that believes in homework
"It's important" you hear them say
This group is known by all of us,
we refer to them as THEY

THEY are for lots of homework,
THEY know it is what's BEST
THEY can't back their beliefs by research,
But that doesn't stop their quest.

THEY think all good teachers,
assign homework every day.
THEY support strict mandates
that don't allow much time for play.

THEY are usually the reason
systems are filled with flaws,
Because we often do what THEY say
without a legitimate cause.

So take heed all ye educators,
view homework in a NEW LIGHT.
Remember, a new direction's needed
THEY are not always right!

Neila A. Connors

References Cited in Text

Arth, Alfred A., & Olsen, M. (1980, February). How To Assign Homework. *Middle School Journal*, 4-5 & 15.

Bergenski, M.D. (1988). A surefire cure for kids who hate homework. *Learning, 17* (8), 91-92

Bergstrom, J. (1985). Letter home about homework. *Instructor, 95* (3), 78-80.

Bradshaw, J. (1985). *Homework: Helping students achieve.* Arlington, VA: American Association of School Administrators.

Buzan, T. (1984). *Make the most of your mind.* NY: E.P. Dutton, p. 59.

Cooper, H.M. (1989). *Homework.* White Plains, NY: Longman

Council on Middle Level Education. (1985) *An agenda for excellence at the middle level.* Reston, VA: National Association of Secondary School Principals.

England, D.A., & Flately, J.K. (1985). *Homework — and why.* Bloomington, Indiana: Phi Delta Kappa Educational Foundation.

Epstein, J.L. (1988). Teacher's reported practice of parent involvement: Problems and possibilities. *Elementary School Journal, 83,* 103-113.

Featherstone, H. (1985). What does homework accomplish? *Principal, 65* (2), 6-7.

Friesen, C.D. (1979). The results of homework vs. no homework research studies. *ERIC Digest.* ED167503

Foyle H.C., & Bailey, G.D. (1988). Research homework experiments in social studies: Implications for teaching. *Social Education, 52*(4), 296-298.

Garvin, J. (1990). *A sane transition to the middle school program.* Rowley, MA: Garvin Consultant Services, p. 47.

Horner, C.M. (1987). Homework: A way to teach problem solving. *Academic Therapy, 22,* 239-244.

Keith, R. (1986). *Homework*. West Lafayette, Indiana: Kappa Delta Pi.

Langdon, G., & Stout, I.W. (1969). *Homework*. New York: John Day Company.

Lee, J.F., & Pruitt, K.W. (1979). Homework assignments: Classroom games or teaching tools? *Clearing House, 53,* 31-35.

Lounsbury, John H. (1989, March). Homework — is a new direction needed? *Middle School Journal, 23.*

O'Donnell, H. (1985). Homework in the elementary school. *Reading Teacher, 80,* 726-732.

Oppenheim, J. (1989, September). Kids, parents, and homework. *Good Housekeeping,* 148 & 165.

Partin, R.L. (1986). Homework that helps. *Clearing House 60*(3), 118-119.

Paschal, R.A. (1984). Effects of homework on learning: A quantative synthesis. *Journal of Educational Research, 78*(2), 97-104.

Salend, S.J., & Schliff, J. (1988). The many dimensions of homework. *Acedemic Therapy,* 23 (4), 397-403.

Schurr, Sandra (1989). *Dynamite in the classroom: A how-to handbook for teachers.* Columbus, OH: National Middle School Association, p. 63.

Strother, D.B. (1984). Homework: Too much, just right, or not enough? *Education Week, 3*(36), 423-427.

Theroux, P. (1988, October). First, do your homework. *Parents,* 53-59.

Turvey, J.S. (1986) Homework — its importance to student achievement. *NASSP Bulletin, 70,* 27-35.

Vardell, S.M. (1987, May/June). Working with parents to help students write. *Learning,* 48-49.

Walberg, H.J., Paschal, R.A., & Weinstein, T. (1985). Homework's powerful effects on learning. *Educational Leadership, 42*(7), 76-79.

Additional Resources on Homework

Baer, T. (1987). Gathering and sharing for homework. *English Journal, 76(4),* 79-80.

Barber, B. (1986). Homework does not belong on the agenda for educational reform. *Educational Leadership, 43,* 55-57.

Bonfiglio, J.F. (1988). Evolution of a model homework policy and practice statement.

Burns, M. (1986). Does math make good homework? *Instructor, 96,* 92–97.

Canter, L. (1989). *Creative Homework.* Santa Monica, CA: Lee Canter & Associates, Inc.

Canter, L. (1988). Homework without tears. *Instructor, 98,* 28-30.

Canter L. & Hausner, L. (1987) *Homework without tears.* New York: Harper & Row Publishers.

Chen, C., & Stevenson, H.W. (1989). Homework: A cross-cultural examination. *Child Development, 60(3),* 551-560.

Clark, F. & Clark, C. (1989) *Hassle-free homework.* New York: New York.

Clary, L.M. (1986) Help for the homework hassle. *Academic Therapy, 22,* 57-60.

Corbishley, M.A., & Yost, E.B. (1985). Therapeutic homework assignments. *The School Counselor, 33,* 57-61.

Coulter, F. (1979). Homework: A neglected research area. *British Educational Research Journal, 5(1),* 21-33.

Foyle, H.C. (1986). Homework: The connection between school and home. *NASSP Bulletin, 70,* 36-38.

Foyle, H.C., & Bailey, G.D. (1986). Homework: Its real purpose. *Clearing House, 60,* 187-188.

Homing in on homework. *Phi Delta Kappan* (1989), *70,* 732-733.

Ivey, J. (1988). No excuses. *Learning, 16*(9), 88.

Jongsma, E. (1985). Research views — homework: Is it worthwhile? *Reading Teacher, 38*(7), 702-704.

Keith, T.Z. (1982). Time spent on homework and high school grades: A large sample path analysis. *Journal of Educational Psychology, 75,* 248-253.

Keith, T.Z., Reimers, T.M., Fehrmann, P.G., Pottebaum, S.M., & Aubey, L.W. (1986). Parental involvement, homework, and TV time: Direct and indirect effects on high school achievement. *Journal of Educational Psychology, 78,* 373-380.

Knorr, C.L. (1981). *A systhesis of homework research and related literature.* Paper presented to the Lehigh Chapter of Phi Delta Kappa in Bethlehem, PA. (ERIC Document Reproduction Service ED 199 933).

Koch, A. (1988). Creative and communicative homework. *Hispania, 71*(3), 699-704.

LaConte, R.R. (ed). (1981). *Homework as a learning experience: What research says to the teacher.* Washington, DC: National Education Association. (ED 217022)

LaConte, R.R. & Doyle, M.A. (1986). *Homework as a learning experience.* Washington, DC: National Education Association.

McDill, E.L., & Natriello, G. (1986). Performance standards, student effort on homework, and academic achievement. *Sociology of Education, 59,* 18-31.

Moskowitz, F.C. (1988). Help parents boost kids' study skills. *Executive Education, 10*(9), 26.

Orsetti, S. (1984). Ideas in practice: Mathematics homework in the classroom. *Journal of Developmental & Remedial Education, 8*(2), 22-23.

Palardy, J.M. (1988). The effect of homework policies on student achievement. *NASSP Bulletin, 72,* 14-17.

Pendergrass, R.A. (1985). Homework: Is it really a basic? *Clearing House, 58*(7), 310-314.

Rosenberg, M.S. (1988). The effects of daily homework assignments on the acquisition of basic skills by students with learning disabilities. *Journal of Learning Disabilities,22*(5), 314-323.

Searls, D.T., Mead, N.A., & Ward, B. (1985). The relationship of students' reading skills to TV watching, leisure time reading, and homework. *Journal of Reading, 29,* 158-162.

Singh, B. (1987). Homework and homework hotlines: Views of junior high school students, teachers, and parents. *ERS Spectrum, 5,* 14-18.

Stewart, J. (1989, February). The homework dilemma. *Parents,* 80-85.

Swartz, L.K. (1986). A DRAB way to remember assignments. *Journal of Reading, 30,* 265.

Tamir, P. (1985). Homework and science learning in secondary schools. *Science Education, 69,* 605-618.

Williams, M.S. (1988, September). Help your kids get a handle on homework. *McCalls,* 52.

Appendix
HOMEWORK SURVEY

Please complete the following:
Check one: ___Male ___Female
Position: ___teacher ___administrator ___parent
___professor ___counselor ___media specialist
Other (please specify position) _____
How many years have you been working with teaching early adolescents?_____
State where you teach: _____ School _____

Everyone is to answer the following questions:
1. Do you feel that students should be given homework (next to each grade level please specify the total number of minutes per night the student should be working on all homework assignments)?
   in the 4th grade? __yes __no total # of minutes _____
   in the 5th grade? __yes __no total # of minutes _____
   in the 6th grade? __yes __no total # of minutes _____
   in the 7th grade? __yes __no total # of minutes _____
   in the 8th grade? __yes __no total # of minutes _____

The following questions refer to students in grades 6-8:
2. Do you feel that students should have homework
   on weekends? ___yes ___no ___sometimes
   on holidays? ___yes ___no ___sometimes
   every week-night (Mon-Thur)? ___yes ___no
3. Do you think that parents should help their children with their homework assignments? ___yes ___no ___sometimes
4. Do you think that all students in a class should do the same assignment? ___yes ___no ___sometimes
5. Do you think that students should exchange papers and grade each others'? ___yes ___no ___sometimes
6. Do you think that **every** assignment should count as a grade? ___yes ___no
7. Should teachers personally grade and comment on **every** homework assignment? ___yes ___no ___sometimes
8. Should homework assignments be coordinated with other teachers in the same grade to avoid "homework overload?" ___yes ___no ___sometimes
9. How much should homework count toward the final grade in the class?
   ___10% ___15% ___25% ___50% ___75%
   ___100% ___Other (please specify___)

10. Should students be punished if they do not complete homework assignments? ___yes ___no ___sometimes
11. Should homework be used for
    punishment? ___yes ___no ___sometimes
    extra credit? ___yes ___no ___sometimes
    slow students only?___yes ___no ___sometimes
    retention? ___yes ___no ___sometimes
12. Should homework be
    corrected? ___always ___sometimes
    reviewed/graded in class? ___always ___sometimes
    planned? ___always ___sometimes
    reviewed/explained thoroughly
        during the class time ___always ___sometimes
    displayed? ___always ___sometimes
13. Do you think that completing homework increases a student's academic achievement?___never ___sometimes

Only persons presently teaching and assigning homework— please complete the following section:
subject(s) teaching _____grade level(s) _____
# of students teaching per day _____Are you on a team? _____
Do you give homework to your students? _____yes _____no
If Yes please answer the following:
14. Do you coordinate homework assignments with other teachers?___yes ___no ___sometimes
15. What type of homework assignment do you assign **most often?** ____ practice _____ preparation
        _____ extension _____ creative
16. Do you assign "group homework assignments?" (students can work together) ___yes ___no ___sometimes
17. Approximate the % of students, per class that complete homework assignments on time _____
18. Please explain any <u>exciting</u> and/or <u>innovating</u> homework assignments (on a separate sheet of paper) that students
Optional: School Address: _____
Name _____Phone:_____
Can I use your comments as quotes in the monograph? _____

Please return the questionnaire **by March 1, 1990** to: Neila A. Connors, Department of Middle Grades, Education Center, Valdosta State College, Valdosta, Georgia 31698. tel: 912-333-5611 or 904-562-1959

Publications
NATIONAL MIDDLE SCHOOL ASSOCIATION

Exploration: The Total Curriculum, Mary F. Compton, Horace C. Hawn (192 pages)

Involving Families in Middle Level Education, John Myers, Luetta Monson (48 pages)

Connecting the Curriculum Through Interdisciplinary Instruction, John H. Lounsbury, Editor (168 pages)

How to Evaluate Your Middle School, Sandra L. Schurr (86 pages)

Nurturing a Teacher Advisory Program, Claire G. Cole (54 pages)

This We Believe, National Middle School Association (40 pages)

The ABC's of Evaluation—26 Alternative Ways to Assess Student Progress, Sandra Schurr (232 pages)

Treasure Chest, Cheryl Hoversten, Nancy Doda, John Lounsbury (268 pages)

Homework: A New Direction, Neila A. Connors (104 pages)

Professional Preparation and Certification, National Middle School Association (24 pages)

On Site: Preparing Middle Level Teachers Through Field Experiences, Deborah A. Butler, Mary A. Davies, and Thomas S. Dickinson (84 pages)

As I See It, John H. Lounsbury (112 pages)

The Team Process: A Handbook for Teachers, Third and enlarged edition, Elliot Y. Merenbloom (173 pages)

Life Stories: The Struggle for Freedom and Equality in America, Lynn L. Mortensen, Editor (166 pages)

Education in the Middle Grades: Overview of National Practices and Trends, Joyce L. Epstein and Douglas J. Mac Iver (92 pages)

Middle Level Programs and Practices in the K-8 Elementary School: Report of a National Study, C. Kenneth McEwin and William M. Alexander (46 pages)

A Middle School Curriculum: From Rhetoric to Reality, James A. Beane (84 pages)

Visions of Teaching and Learning: Eighty Exemplary Middle Level Projects, John Arnold, Editor (160 pages)

The New American Family and the School, J. Howard Johnston (48 pages)

The Japanese Junior High School: A View from the Inside, Paul S. George (56 pages)

Schools in the Middle: Status and Progress, William M. Alexander and C. Kenneth McEwin (112 pages)

A Journey Through Time: A Chronology of Middle Level Resources, Edward J. Lawton (36 pages)

Dynamite in the Classroom: A How-To Handbook for Teachers, Sandra L. Schurr (272 pages)

Developing Effective Middle Schools Through Faculty Participation, Second and enlarged Edition, Elliot Y. Merenbloom (122 pages)

Guidance in Middle Level Schools: Everyone's Responsibility, Claire G. Cole 30 pages

Preparing to Teach in Middle Level Schools, William M. Alexander and C. Kenneth McEwin (64 pages)

Young Adolescent Development and School Practices: Promoting Harmony, John Van Hoose and David Strahan (68 pages)

When the Kids Come First: Enhancing Self-Esteem, James A. Beane and Richard P. Lipka (96 pages)

Interdisiciplinary Teaching: Why and How, Gordon F. Vars (56 pages)

The Middle School, Donald H. Eichhorn (128 pages)

Positive Discipline: A Pocketful of Ideas, William Purkey and David Strahan (56 pages)

Adviser-Advisee Programs: Why, What, and How, Michael James (75 pages)

Evidence for the Middle School, Paul George and Lynn Oldaker (52 pages)

Perspectives: Middle Level Education, John H. Lounsbury, Editor (190 pages)

VIDEOTAPE

Success With Discipline: The Trials of Jenny Tippet, A video-supported in-service program on managing behavior in the middle level classroom, 3 videos and comprehensive training guide. Call NMSA for a free brochure.

National Middle School Association
4807 Evanswood Drive
Columbus, Ohio 43229-6292
614-848-8211   FAX 614-848-4301